Third Edition

ISBN: 979 8393256487

Printed in the U.S.A

The Forgotten War of 1950

In Their Adolescence

Remembered by 8 Octogenarians

Third Edition

An anthology of vivid and elegiac remembrances of

The Forgotten War by eight Koreans who witnessed

The tragedy and destruction of the Korean War of

1950 in their teens.

Chang-Wuk Kang, M.D.

Se-Woong Ro

Editors

In Memory

of

Professor Yearn Hong Choi

2023

The Introduction by The Creator for the First Edition

An Anthology of vivid and elegiac remembrance of the Korean War as recalled by eight senior citizens who, as eight young children in 1950-1953, witnessed the tragedy and destruction of the so called "Forgotten War."

The Korean War has been forgotten, but it should not be. One American citizen registered his complaint in the Washington Post's opinion page about the news paper's silence on the 70th anniversary of the war (Charles McGovern, Free for All page, July 19, 2020). Thankfully, Washington Post columnist George Will posted a touching story (Thanksgiving 2020) about a Korean War veteran who survived the massive Chinese attacks of the Chosin Reservoir.

This book is dedicated to the memories of the Korean War. History should be remembered. If not, human civilization cannot progress.

February 2021

Yearn Hong Choi and Bernard Rowan,

The first editors.

Preface

On June 25, 1950, early in the morning, the North Korean army crossed the 38th parallel with massive armament, such as the Russian tanks and 105mm Field Howitzer. The unannounced stealth attack was the beginning of the massive destruction of the Korean peninsula, not to mention the loss of millions of lives. Already the South Korea was one of the poorest countries just recovered from the Japanese annexation for 36 years. To any eyes, the land became a hopelessly ashen as the North Korean reached near the downstream of Nakdong River cornering the defensive south Korean forces and small allied forces. To any historian, it was miracle that the south Korean was able to hold back the invader with the persistent stalemate along the Nakdong River. That was enough time for the newly created allied forces, under the Command of General MacArthur of the United States of America, were able to prepare counter attacks and even invade the north by landing operation on the Inchon harbor which cut off the northern forces trapped in the south to be isolated by the mid-September 1950. Allied forces recovered the entire peninsula including the northern part of the Korean peninsula by very fast push by the allied forces, mostly by American forces in a couple of months. It was but a short period. As expected, the Chinese involvement of the war became real and this massive Chinese infantry, so called Chinese People's Volunteer Army was able to stop the allied forces immediately at the northern border of the peninsula, along the Yalu and Duman rivers in late October 1950. The number of Chinese troops was so large that it was simply called 'human sea waves.' Some estimates were a million. For the few months while the Chinese pushed to the south, they lost 920,000 soldiers. It also was reported that not every Chinese soldier were armed properly either. Nothing could prevent the movement of the massive human waves. At last, they pushed back the allied forces to the middle of the peninsula and then eventually the front line fell in stalemate along the current border, close to the original 38th parallel. At last, the infamous armistice was signed between the representations of the allied forces and the North Korean Chinese side on July 27, 1953. The sound of guns was silenced by the armistice at last, and it has been held so far for the past 70 years. But the tragedy of people trapped on both sides became permanent strangers for a long time. The separation of many Korean families by the division of the peninsular for the past 70 years, it's one's lifetime, and the sorrow of the nation by the separation of so many families has been indescribable human tragedy. One of my close friends left three of his sisters when he took refuge in the south at his teens, about 14 years of age. I cannot ask him about it without evoking his pain. This is the second such tragedy of the people of Korea. The first was massive separation of the Korean due to the Japanese occupation in the 20th century. There was huge human migration from Korean peninsula to the Manchuria, Eastern Russia and then to the Central Asia, initially by the Japanese occupation and then by the USSR under the Starlin's control for forceful farming labor in the central Asia. I wonder how the folks of Korea have known in their heart and talking about it; as their fate accepting passively as the history of several separations of the people of Korea. One of the most famous Korean folk songs 'Arirang' is about the separation of lovers.

The reconstruction following the armistice of the Korean War started in the south earnestly but somewhat tediously as the destruction was so devastatingly massive and the Korea was one of the poorest countries in the world, even with massive assistance from overseas, mainly from United States. The common expression of the state of Republic of Korea (still some call her South Korea) was pile of ashes.

There was a nation called Chosen on the Korean peninsula until the end of 19th century. Her name was changed to Daehan Empire during the reign of the last Emperor of the Chosen Dynasty, KoJong in mid-19th century. The history of Chosen for the first half century was tumultuous and the country was barely able to stand until Japan simply walked out of the country as they surrendered to the United States on August 15, 1945. Until then, somehow, she was able to repel many invasions even though the country was weak in defense. By the middle of the 19the century the country became helplessly weak, and it did not take much effort for the Japanese Empire to annex the country by colonizing the peninsula in 1919 winning the competition between Japan, China, and Russia. The Japanese occupation lasted until the end of the World War II when Japan surrendered to United States on August 15, 1945. We still called the day 'The Day of Emancipation.' But sadly, the peninsula was divided into two regions, the South Korea and the North Korea, along the dividing line of the 38th parallel. by the decision quite arbitrarily made between the United States and the USSR. Why the 38th parallel? Who knows. But it just appeared to be reasonable half and half in size of the land. It sounded rather random haphazard decision by someone representing the USA and the USSR. The dividing line was simply cutting the waist of the peninsular right in the middle. After a political tumult in Korea, the south was able to obtain recognition by the United Nation as 'The Republic of Korea'. The southern half of Korea became a democratic nation by her constitution; with a constitution that is very western in flavor. It readily used the word 'God' 'Freedom' despite culturally and religiously the Korea was close to the more Buddhism and Confucianism. The north Korea was to become 'The Democratic People's Republic of Korea' and she was also recognized universally through the becoming a member of United Nation. But there was very little democracy in structure and governance in the north. None can deny that it is a totalitarian nation by the dictatorial power of Kim Il-sung family from the beginning. This is a much worse tragedy for the Korean people, and this book is the story based on the conflict between these differences of the divided nation to two nations.

The growth of Republic of Korea as a democratic nation and industrialization speeded up after the military coup in 1961. In 1988 the Korea (Republic of Korea) was even able to open 88th Universal Olympic in Seoul, Korea quite successfully. That was when many people in the world learned there was a little country called the Republic of Korea. She became the 4th largest economy in Asia and 10th largest in the world by the time entering 21st century. The country is about one third of Japan and very tiny to compare with China. Like the expression of the 'The Miracle of the Rhine' for the advancement of the German economy, some call the advancement of the Korean economy as 'The Miracle on The Han River.' About 12 years ago, I had a fortune to take a vacation in Europe touring three countries, Austria, Hungary and Czechoslovakia. I was pleasantly surprised by the ubiquity of billboards of Korean products. Those young people on the street were so kind to us and did not seem to mind spending a few minutes to guide us the directions we asked. This was stark contrast to what I experienced when I arrived in Unites States in 1965, they had no idea where Korea was located even after so many of their young people were sacrificed during the Korean war. So-called yellow people were strangers to them. Meanwhile, I have encountered many news and stories about what Korean have been doing to express their gratitude to the nations who helped the Republic of Korea during the Korean war and reconstruction effort of Korea. An old person who can barely move around was seen on the TV screen in his home in Ethiopia. The poverty was obvious. He was one of the soldiers volunteered to help in the Korean war as an allied troop during the war. I was so grateful and emotional when I came across the story of what the Korean people look for the opportunity to express their gratitude for those who helped in Korean war and the development. The space is not enough to list such efforts by the Koreans to so many people of the world who helped Korea to grow to become what she is now. I am so grateful for the fact that Koreans never forget gratitude. But all the writers of this book believe that if you do not know the facts, how can you show proper expression of gratitude?

The thought has been in my mind, and I believe many Koreans have so too. But if you do not know what you are grateful for how can you exercise to express your gratitude? It became apparent to me that some people wished to forget the war and create their own personal history in their mind. I suspect that it may not last too long before you will find why you are in where you are, the 'truth". The number of those who know and remember about the Korean War is decreasing fast. Thus, we do need to know the facts around our lives. The Korean war came and gone, but we have been affected by the war initially with tragedy, then lesson and then hope and strength. So, we need to know where we were, how we came from where we are, and what and how we should move from what we learn.

I wish that learning from the history of the Korean war from those who experienced it we can find precious lessons that can help our way to see the present and future. I am hoping that this anthology is part of such an effort in progress. I am so grateful that we can meet those who still have vivid memories of their encounter with the Korean tragedy. I have very little doubt that this book will serve the purpose. Finally, I am so grateful for the writers who readily accepted the invitation to contribute the stories from their precious memories of that took place in their teen age during the Korean war. I am also mostly grateful for the initiation of the idea and initiation of the project of this volume by Professor Se-Woong Ro for this volume; shall I say the entire project is his brainchild. I am also very grateful for the initiation of the project in publishing the first book about young people 's experience of the Korean War at the very first volume in 2021 by the Late Professor Yearn Hon Choi, rest in peace.

Finally, I am very grateful to all the contributors for their part in this anthology.

Editor

March 15, 2023

The Contents

Introductions for this edition

The authors of this book are all educated at graduate school level and so were their professional careers. Several of them carry teaching positions in post graduate education.

Mr. Yong Kyun Lim, after graduating from Kyung Hee University he dedicated in broadcasting system in Korea, including the Voice of America. The high light of his career includes the invitation to the State Department of United States for a month.

Dr. Hie-Won Lee Hann, M.D. graduated from Seoul National University College of Medicine and has been a faculty of Thomas Jefferson University Hospital, in Philadelphia, as Director of Liver Disease Prevention Center. She is the highest expert in the world in 'B Hepatitis' which has been mostly prevalent in East Asia. I believe most of the adult Korean should remember the horrors of the B Hepatitis. With the leadership of Dr. Hann the scourge almost disappeared from the Korean peninsula. I wonder how may know this fact.

Dr. Richard Suhung Hann was the Director of Pediatric Immunology at the Hahnemann Medical College in Philadelphia.

Mr. Kyung-Joo Lee was born in North Korea and passed away in recent past after he made the contribution of his articles for this book. May he rest in peace! He was a poet and contributed large numbers of poems about Korean War veterans published. He received numerous awards and recognitions.

Dr. Seung-Kyoon Park graduated from Seoul National University College of Medicine. He served as the Director of Outpatient Psychiatry at the University of Buffalo, Jacob School of Medicine, and Biomedical Science as a professor in psychiatry. He is like a monument in the clinic.

Dr. Paul Pyung Sung, M.D. graduated from Korea University College of Medicine. He is an ordained elder of the Methodist Church.

Dr. Eungshik Won, Ph.D. has the unique nickname as 'Mushroom Doctor' as the Ph.D. in Agriculture. He also has blackbelt level in Taekwondo. He is a member of Korean Peaceful Unification Advisory Committee along with numerous public services, many for the Korean and Korean American.

Dr. Chang-Wuk Kang assists in editing this book. He has been a psychiatrist for the past 50 years in America and is a graduate of Seoul National University Medical college.

Chang-Wuk Kang

Editor

A New Road

Yong Kyun Lim

Having Lost Two Brothers of Mine!

Bro! My little brother!

I am an octogenarian, but I still get tearful from time to time when I miss my two brothers, one older and the other younger than I was. It may sound like a little child, but I do feel like a little child when I am drawn into the memory of the yester years, by calling their names loudly in my heart. It is hard to get out of the yearning and even crying, not just being tearful but sometimes I do cry openly and loudly when I am alone. It is hard to control and to calm myself down when I am drawn into the memory by whatever is triggered. Sometimes I don't know what to do with myself. Regardless whose fault it was, my brothers who died in the Korean War, called '625 War' in Korea, cannot come back to life. I am too aware of it. Every year on this day, June the 25th, I cannot help but to shed tears as I cannot help but to think about my lost brothers. Usually, I end up getting the hateful thought about the war. I could not help but recall what happened to them, my brothers' demise. I do not know what to do about the memories of them. Sometimes I wish I could forget about it. I have tried to forget about them but then I noticed that at times I am intentionally trying to recall them. I have been trying to work very hard paying attention to my daily life, but I could not help but to be drawn into the sorrowful memories about them. I wonder everyone who lost his or her beloved by the war go through the same. It just does not go away. But then, I am not trying to forget either as I said, and this conflict comes more so on the 25th of month of June, every year.

Lately, watching the news coming from around the world on the TV news hours, particularly such scenes where I see young boys and girls separated from their family in the chaos of the war zones. I am forced to recall our history of the war. I aspire not to have war. I even fantasize such as creating such system or organization as a system of the deterrence index that can function like a deterrence to the war and the human rights violations. Some systems are made in the effort to prevent corrupt national leaders triggering such violence and some systems are forming anti-war networks that gather the public opinion of peace-loving people by the digital connections encompassing the world. All countries in the world have pure private organizations like 'non-governmental' in which ordinary people can participate. Oh, yes! It may be a very naïve idea, as if it has not been tried. Even if you may create one like that, I wonder if it can be powerful enough to carry out such a difficult task, like what we are watching and what is taking place in the world. Someone said such a dream does not cost a penny but would require enormous commitment and effort.

To prevent the violence and the tragedies arising from the result of the horrific war, the facts and truth must be accurately recorded. So that, a clear and definite, and tangible historical condemnation must be carried out. Even when one survey the result of the Korean War, it is quite regrettable that many people, particularly younger generations who did not physically experienced war, are not properly learning the accurate history of what really took place as there are many of those who are trying to cover up the truth, even still.

* * *

The Korean War started on June 25, 1950, early in the morning by the undeclared invasion by the North Korea. The result was unspeakably severe devastation on the Korean peninsula. Over

1.2 million were dead by the war at the silence of the gun sounds. The destruction of the land, both south and north across the dividing line, was such that the whole country was covered by destruction and ashes. The war brought military forces from 16 of the UN member countries. The forces of the United States lead the U.N Forces and fought against the northern communist forces. The war was devastating, by not only having inflicted many lives but also left the country in ashes virtually, amid the shadow of the Cold War that divided the left and the right ideologies into two groups of the nation's lead by the two great powers, USA, and USSR.

Today, Korea is attracting the attention of all over the world. One reason is that Korea not only survived the devastation by the war, but also has been able to serve as an anti-communist bastion facing the expansion by the international communist powers. And, while trying to overcome such severe adversity, after the armistice established Korea has shown a remarkable national resilience and efforts to achieve the steady and fast growth in many aspects, not only industrial growth but also cultural demonstration. For example, once the totally unknown language of Korea became a popular second language to the world, particularly among the young and intellectuals started to enjoy it. Furthermore, she is entering into the ranks of the advanced countries, economically and scientifically.

As history shows and, as they say, the greater the fruitage one wishes to achieve, the more misery and pains one must go through. The spirit of the Korean leaders and the blood-stained efforts of the Korean people set the model around the world. I am proud of the Korean national competence. Particularly, the young generation of Korean has shown to the world with various aspects of their gifts such as cultural activities, technical achievements, the competition in sports, and so forth with their pure proud efforts. I believe that it is due to the innate resilience and quiet trust in one's effort. If this true historical fact is not to be passed on to future generations truthfully, it will be judged by history and will never be tolerated. As a person who lived in the north of the 38 parallel at the time of the war broke, which was the border between the two Koreas at the time, I would like to add 'the truth' to the part of the history of this war by writing this story entitled '6.25 War.'

In the spring of 1950—I was 11 years old, living north of the 38th parallel of the Korean peninsula, in Hwacheon, Gangwon-do. I was in the 4th grade of elementary school.

New Road

The distance between my home and the elementary school was less than 1.24 miles. The road was newly paved and widened. We called it New Road and we enjoyed running on the newly paved road up and down as soon as the road was completed. When the automobile started to run in the country, the main road of town and villages started to be widened and paved. The new road was constructed by the labor of the town folks with the government supplies. The new road of my village started from Hwacheon Power Plant to Pungsan-ri in the north, to Geumseong Fortress, which was connected to Mount Geumgangsan, also called the Diamond Mountain, the famous scenic mountain, a little further away. Originally, it used to be a narrow road barely enough for the passage of the cattle. Then, the road was widened enough for the automobiles to pass. It took less than two years to widen and pave the road. In the previous year, as though anything serious might happen, the town authority urged the folks in town to pave the road further even though it was the busy farming season. I said 'urged' but it was de facto 'forced hard labor.'

The rumor that the North Korean army was coming back came to be true. The cold weather in the early winter stayed for several days continuously. My older brother opened the back door of the house and entered in the same shape as before, taking advantage of the darkness of the moonless night, as if he had promised before. He again left the ranks of the South Korean security forces as the unit was withdrawing to the south as the northern troop was pushing to the south in the dead winter. He looked anxious pacing restlessly in the room as if he was looking for something or trying to figure out what to do with some problem.

He called my mother. She was about to go to the place my father was staying to discuss the situation of my home and the village. He said he was thinking hurriedly too. The story he revealed was that the remnants of the People's Army of North Korea were already forming their ranks in the northern mountainous area, the South Korean Army had been already ordered to withdraw, and the South Korean security personnel whom my maternal uncle used to work for left for the south already. He could not imagine that he couldn't go to the south alone, leaving his older brother behind. Also, there was nothing I could say to my brother on Mother's Day, who always believed my home was the safest place. No matter how much the world changed by the progress of the world, we stayed and lived in that slanted thatched house. I didn't know which world was supposed to be good or which people were right, between the south and the north. The country was mercilessly cut in the middle of the peninsula right in the middle along the 38th parallel into two nations in the south and the north. They are all ignorant as far as I was concerned, so when they are scared, sad or lonely, the only place one can crawl into seeking warm protection was the bosom of the family.

All night long, my family kept discussing about how to escape the unbearable situation and get away from the village as though that might have been the only solution, but my older brother, knowing that he could not leave his family in this home behind, was starting to calculate in his head looking for a solution, a reasonable solution. He must have felt like he was losing his mind as he imagined that the chances of his survival at the time were only half and a half of what should have been best odd. Then, he changed his mind again and was about to decide that he should run away all by himself, and so forth. But he just could not make up his mind. He went back and forth, again and again. But whatever my brother's decision might have been, good or bad, it was to come certainly. The sadness of leaving his mother and family behind and the fear of being caught and executed were constantly intruding in his mind, and my head too. My brother must have prepared in his mind resolutely that if he were captured by the North Korean soldiers he would be tortured, or he would suffer very little doubt. The defector of the North Korean People's Army, worked as a security guard for the South Korean side, would without doubt be judged as a crime of treason. And one cannot imagine what kind of punishment would be imposed on such persons. We all felt helpless thinking about such a predicament. None looks hopeful. All the family were downcast only looking at the empty floor, as if everyone was hanging on the edge of a cliff hopelessly.

At last, late in the morning, several North Korean soldiers appeared in town. Two from the group of soldiers started surveying the village, checking the houses one by one. One of them went in and out of the private gate of a house that was bordering the outskirts. When an old woman saw one of the

North Korean soldiers holding his gun high as if he was aiming at something. She approached one of the soldiers and begged. "No. Please! We have a child" she begged. It sounded like she was saying 'save me,' as she was muttering as she was so frightened as though the gun was pointed at her. Then, one of the soldiers standing behind a pole near the door of the house shouted toward the rooms of the house. "Raise all your hands with the weapons high, and then come out slowly." My brother had no weapons. The soldier was quite agile in dealing with any suspect or enemy. My brother raised his hands like he was surrendering and came out of the room. The soldier shouted at my brother; "Hey you! You …! Get down!" slamming my brother's shoulder with the rifle buttstock. My brother fell on his face, instinctively uttering "hey!" The soldier stepped into the room which my brother was hiding just a few minutes earlier. Finding out there was no weapon and nothing else in the room the soldier shouted at my brother again questioning something.

At this moment, the soldier standing outside of the house sent a signal toward the public hall, shouting "stay there a minute." He then summoned the other soldiers who were inside the house as if something urgently needed to be taken care of. Then, he just went away hurriedly. The People's Army headquarters was set up in the public hall of the town. Two soldiers came from there and dragged my brother away at last.

About midday, the messenger from the People's Army came to the village. The voice of the announcement was with low tone, but stern as can be and frightening even; 'you will be shot as a traitor. So, don't approach the scene.' All the families soon started weeping and wailing. The whole place became an ocean of tears. As expected, we were helpless, and that was all we could expect and there was no helpful idea under the circumstance. My mother, who followed them from her house, weeping and the tears were dropping on the cold bare ground. When she returned, I had to take her duvet and wrap me and my mother. My grandmother walked into her room first with her sister, one of my aunts who gestured to me to help my mother to the room. No one approached our house and a few moments later the place became deadly quiet at last.

During the night, the sporadic sounds of gunshots were heard. The sounds were like those of rifles. The sound seemed to be coming from the power plant, about 40 miles away. The gunshots were heard repeatedly for a while and then silence followed. When it resumed it then became for longer period, for several hours, as though they were entering into a kind of a state of new order. My grandmother and my mother were worried about how to collect the body of their child as though death of their child was certain, although my mother was silent. She was up all night in tears. My grandmother went to the front of the private gate of the house early in the morning as though she was waiting for someone. It was certain that she was hoping for any message about her grandson's where about and if he might come. She stared at the public hall motionlessly. The building was about a hundred meters in distance. She then suddenly called me out of the room of the house in a hushed but urgent voice. She pointed with her finger to a soldier in a People's Army uniform, staggering toward them. Alas, it was her grandson, and my mother's oldest son; the son who should have been killed certainly by the North Korean soldier in their imagination. As soon as he saw me, he gestured to me to come to him closer. I approached him quickly. It certainly was him and I let him lean on me by holding my shoulder. He could barely walk now. I could not help but burst into tears. Rather, my older brother was trying to comfort me, saying "you shouldn't cry" in a tired and weak voice. I could barely hear him. My brother's physical condition was such that he was on the verge of giving away. I knew how harsh the interrogation by the Red Army was like. I had been beaten many times by the North Korean soldiers myself, but also, I have been subjected to various kinds of tortures when they interrogated me whatever information they wanted to squeeze out of me. It was even heard that, instead of shooting the victim, at times the senior officers of the North Korean soldiers sometime gave the order to stop the interrogations and torture and send the victims to the front line of the war. The fighting around the power plant must have been unfavorable for the North Korean People's Army as they were short of men, and they could not help but becoming the helplessly trapped targets by the allied forces.

There was nothing much the family could offer other than let the older brother rest. We found out that before he could rest enough and stay with us enough, he had to leave us early in the morning to report to the local headquarters of the North Korean People's Army. A long gun was already hung on his drooped shoulder no sooner the daybreak arrived.

In the south, about 30 miles from the town, apparently a fierce battle was taking place. We also heard rumors. Then, the roar of the gunfire from Hwacheon Power Plant became gradually louder. My brother now held the rifle hanging tight on his shoulder, but it was nothing but to put into use for a bullet holder. He was taken away by a soldier of the People's Army to some place for his certain execution, that we could not help but to believe.

*   *   *

In the spring of 1950, I was 11 years old, living in the north of the 38th parallel in Hwacheon, Gangwon-do, that was in

North Korea before the Korean War took place. I was in fourth grade in a local people's school (elementary school under the communist regime). The town of Pungsan-ri, where I lived, belongs to Hwacheon-myeon. It was a rural farming village. I had to cross the Baemeori Pass about 3.7 miles in distance, by the power plant and then the country road 7.4 more miles to be able to reach the town market. It was a time of the spring hunger, so called 'Passage of Barley', the period in the month of March, when it was difficult to live through because of lack of saved grains as the farming villages lack in reserved grains. It had been expected and farmers knew they had to bear with it. On top of this adversity, the town folks were called by the authority to work on the pavement of the road. Anyone can imagine the burden the town folk had to carry out. They had very little energy and they could barely sustain themselves. This was the hardest time of the year for the farmers in the entire rural areas of the country. I believe it was a universal phenomenon all over the world. It was not only difficult time just for the farmers of this country, but also the town people all together, since previous fall, the town peoples seemed to be barely sustaining their hard lives with the frequent mandatory meetings, so-called voluntary activities and mobilizations such as the cleaning up the new roads, the night schools to fight illiteracy, the women's alliance meetings, and so forth under the rule of the Democratic People's Republic of Korea (The North Korean Communist Country). My maternal grandmother, who was the oldest in my family, lamented often saying "I need to make money to live, but I had no time because of the statute meetings and labors. It was for every adult in the village with no exceptions even if you might be sick. How can I live?" My mother lamented incessantly night and day. It was quite a universal murmur and universal agony.

It had been almost two years since my father left for the Soviet Union to find work or to make money as a technician of some sort. In the same month, right after my father left for Soviet, my brother received a conscription order from the People's Army. The family was in the predicament of imminent break up by such glooms piling up. My family had been agonizing over this for some time, but I also had to have my own share of difficult time with the threat of my survival because of my father's claim not to enter my grandfather's house again without his permission. That prevented anything I could find to help the survival of my family. At least that was my belief. However, since we entered my house at the end of April, the same year, a few good things happened to me, something a young person can bear. A few days earlier, I joined the boys' group, which I couldn't join earlier because I couldn't memorize the pledge to pass the test to be accepted to the club and the multiplication table of arithmetic. Since then, I was less anxious about attending the school as I was less intimidated in the school. It was good to have a place to lean on at lunchtime so to speak. Also, I was to dig up grasses or picking up flowers, mostly azalea. When I came home from school, I then waited for the local children gathered in the shape of oak flowers on the hill. I enjoyed doing things together with boys of the village, whatever that might be.

Then, one day, I learned a strange story that apparently spread by the grown-ups in the village as they picked them up by the folks returning from the market in town. Recently, in town, soldiers are moving along the main road by trucks in the night. Also, the countless soldiers, whom we had not seen before, were moving down along the main road extending from north to south, with guns on their shoulders. When dawn approached, it became quiet again as usual. At the center of this a story were the rumors that the world had gone into chaos. It was also true that it became difficult for residents to work during the day as they couldn't sleep at night. There were a lot of murmurs and rumors, but nothing was clear. At the same time, the town people looked with quaint eyes as the North Korean People's Army units, as they have never seen so many soldiers in such short period in the village of the Hwacheon-goon.

As I look back, the spring of 1950 was a time when the Kim Il-Sung's communist regime was secretly rushing to prepare for the invasion of the South Korea by solidifying her system of governance by the so-called 'agitation policies for residents.' In the past there was ideological education only for some of the selected in town but now it is for everyone with the emphasis for strengthening the ideological education, not only for students but also for everybody in North Korea. Even those Soviet troops stationed in North Korea since the end of the World War II, stepped down in their appearance as they gradually started to leave the country. But the teaching of Russian in upper school continued, but not in the elementary school any longer. The singing of the Soviet Union, the birthplace of the Communist Party, was continued in the schools of all levels. Their political analysts said that Soviet leader Joseph Stalin was named Generalissimo, the highest leader, and Kim Il-sung was named General, with the story that he was general when he fought Japanese during the Japanese occupation of Korea and Manchuria. The North Korean regime's support and praise for the Soviet Union even included singing songs praising Moscow. Among the songs, Moscow hymns, Stalin hymns, and Kim Il-sung hymns occupied radio broadcasting all day long in North Korea. At school, innocent children were growing with sort of emotion with sympathy, anger, and so forth as they hear malicious propaganda that the puppet regime, Syngman Rhee, an American imperialist puppet, of the south was oppressing the people of South Korea, and so forth. The propaganda added that the North Koreans must rescue South Korean people as they were the struggling compatriots. The education and propaganda in the school in the North Korea were everything and there was very little education that had nothing to do with the ideology. I remember a scene one summer morning when I was in the third grade. After a light sprinkle, the sky was still cloudy and gloomy. The atmosphere was as gloomy as the weather, and children were forced to line up on the school grounds even though it was one day of the summer vacation of the school. The gathered children were totally quiet. As if catching the seriousness of the situation, the children were gazing in a direction to the south with an alert posture. It was to awaken the children so that they would not fall for the instigation of others like a traitor in the south.

The family of Cheol-Soo, one of my friends, was said to have fled from the village the night before. In Pungsan-ri, his family lived in the house that was the only tiled house with windows in town. Recently, people openly called Cheol-soo's house the 'the home of the landlord reactionary family.' It was around that time that Cheol-soo, who had been the class president for a long time in the school, stepped down from the position. Also, all the fairy tale books were removed, and the cartoons placed on rack on the back wall of the classroom depict the struggles between the strong and the weak and the struggles between the haves and the have-nots. The class struggle it was. These new books depict the contents that arouse hostility toward landowners and capitalists by depicting the main character of the book, such as the robber, the savages, the arrogant behavior of the daughters of a rich family and the wretched image of a girl from a poor family who works hard in the same house, badly treated and so on so forth.

Those who were accused during the last self-criticism after a day of class, were punished with forced digging of the ground for bomb shelters. It was not easy to avoid self-criticism. When the class leader opened with the statement with declaration "I will start the self-criticism time from this moment," anyone was given the right to speak from the chairman and then the accusation began. "Comrade Im OO, please stand up. Why did you curse at me around OO this morning?" I wonder if there is any reason for children's wrestling.

At the 'March First Day' last month, the commemoration of the uprising for the Korean Independence 1919 against Japanese colonial occupation, the representatives of each class of the entire school gave speeches. The content was almost the same as the content of the principal's discourse, but considering the same speech repeated over and over, the purpose seems to be to provoke resentment and agitations. For example, the opening speech of the speeches from 1st to 5th graders all said, "The exploitation and oppression of the Syngman Rhee puppet regime continues today in the southern half of this time when the world situation is complicated and complicated..." As always, the commemoration went into a street march after the keynote speeches. Following the slogan of the class leader (supervisor), "let's overthrow the puppet Syngman Rhee, and rescue the brothers and sisters who are groaning in the gang," the class members chanted in the voices of anger and raised their clenched fists high into the ceilings. I can't remember who said that, but such atmosphere created in the schools and the neighborhood were to emphasize that the people's committees' function was to provoke bare hostility by arousing the thought that we should think of the people of the southern half were oppressed and dying of hunger, thus we must also be able to endure the sorrow and hunger we were experiencing.

It was in mid-May 1950. Various changes were taking place around the area of Hwacheon. On the sandy beach where the stream flowing down from Pungsan-ri meets the main flow of the Bukhan River, the training of cavalry of the People's Army went on every day. For some time, I went up to the hill nearby with friends of mine almost every day to watch the training scenes of cavalry of North Korean soldiers. They were the first group of the cavalry, came down from the north in the springtime. After the group canter, each raced on the horses without the saddle. Since they were running without the saddle, they often fell. It was like learning to become one with the horse when they run by hanging on the neck of the horses from falling. At the same time, the shooting practice was in full swing over the hill behind the power plant, about 5.5 miles away. On the sandy and grassy fields across the river from Hwacheon-eup, the soldiers in camouflage were crawling and training fiercely in the sand and on the grass.

After a few days in Pungsan-ri, even those grown-ups made hubbub by the news of the arrival of an automobile the following day. Children who had never been to town had never seen a car. The children must have had trouble sleeping because they were excited to see a car the next day. Desiring to see a car as closely as possible, we went up to the hilltop by the main road outside Dong-gu, the entrance of the village, where the car should come through. I took a seat behind a tree with many branches so as not to be noticed. I sat down with excitement too, but still some children were scared and tried to hide behind me. At last, the car that was supposed to be coming in the morning showed up around 11 o'clock rolling in with a loud 'bang' sound as if sending a signal that a car was entering Pungsan-ri.

I thought that the roof of the car was a shiny silvery color when it was turning the corner of the foot of the hill, seen from 200 yards, but that was all I saw, and I could not remember anything more. It was only three or four seconds I saw the car, as the car was disappearing from my sight, shaking its heavy body. Later, I heard from village grown-ups that this car was being used to test the efficacy of the newly paved road, and this road was supposed to be made for the military transportation route for the wartime.

***

The full moon passed over the hill. It was in the morning of June 25, 1950, around 5 o'clock. It was Sunday. I was only thinking about the weather as I was looking forward to playing with the kids of the village. I enjoyed with village kids of about my age on Sunday morning. Nothing unusual was expected. Then, there was a sudden loud sound, an explosive sound. It was certainly the loud sound of a cannon fired. It was in fact much louder than the sounds of thunder. It was a dry sunny morning. Then, every few tens of seconds, the explosive sound of heavy cannon seemed to shake the whole ground and the houses. Judging from the fact that all kinds of gunshots sounded like roasting beans on a dry pan, but this was quite different from the smaller guns heard during the training of the soldiers' shooting practice, I should have known. The grandmother of one of my friends in the village said that the gun sounds were coming further from the area of the power plant or from Oeum-ri. The old lady added cautiously by saying, "There is something taking place, some racket perhaps." After all, the older folks were trying to reassure younger folks and children.

Then, I fell asleep again. When I woke up, the weather was clear. There were no loud sounds of guns and only the faint sounds of cannons could be heard intermittently from the distance. I ran down to the front yard of the public hall in the middle of town, hoping to find some kids and play with them. Even from a distance, I could sense some sort of commotion by the movement and expression of the town folks gathered in front of the public hall, murmuring. The children were seen, but the

34

restlessness of the grown-ups was more tangible. Some grown-ups, about ten of them, were standing around a man in their middle. It was the chairman of the People's Committee, and he was eagerly explaining something to those gathered around him. I saw some of the children too, who were also listening to the story with the adults. Then, suddenly they all started to run by the middle of the front yard of the public hall, screaming "Yah-ah" in excitement.

As I too approached the crowds, the father of one of my friends in the village, Mr. Jeon Jeong-gil, chairman of the People's Committee, suddenly raised his hand and started to speak like an exhortation. "Everyone! Now, applaud! Our People's Army is advancing south with successive victories. Let's watch what is taking place." The scroll of paper was spread out and hung on the wall of the public hall. It was the map of Korea. On the map, the 38th parallel line, crossing between Chuncheon and Hwacheon, was drawn, and there were many arrows were drawn along the entire length of the 38-prrarel line pointing to the south. The map was hinting that the occupation of Seoul, the capital of South Korea by the People's Army, was imminent within two or three days.

"This morning, the locally conscripted soldiers of the southern part (South Korean) dare attacked the northern part (North Korean) as though they had no fear. The Korean People's Army, which was attacked unexpectedly by these tentatively conscripted soldiers of the south, immediately and easily repulsed the enemy. By our counterattack we were able to occupy Chuncheon easily. We were able to advance toward further south." The committee's report on the progress of the war was ambiguous and questionable to some, I learned later. In fact, three days after the announcement of the occupation of

Seoul by the committee, the school added new classes for 'the training for arresting spy at night' for the upper-class students, grades 4 and 5, in addition to the traditional ritualistic class and training, even providing them with wooden rifles cut like a toy. Also, they were taught to sing songs to inspire the spirit of patriotism under the slogan 'Brother is on the front line and younger brother is struggle from the rear'. They also started what they called the mental training class, a euphemism for brain washing. About once a month, at 1:00 p.m., one must climb the hill in the rear of the school and was trained to arrest the one who was disguised as enemy infiltrators by the home front. About 12:00 AM, a message was brought by a friend of mine in the village that woke me. I started to run for school. I was very nervous by the loud shouting of the slogan such as 'sisters in the rear' and so forth, then I ran faster and faster. All I can remember was that I was very frightened.

A few days later, the summer vacation ended, and school started earlier than usual. I noticed that there were several boys gathered at the entrance of the classroom. The boy, with the name So-seop, was telling the story that he heard from the boys of the middle school in the village. It was a story about middle school girls who claimed that they were patriotic and rushed to the home office demanding slogans 'give us guns and send us to the front line'. He then raised his voice as he was speaking with a voice of such an excitement, about what he personally witnessed, the whole thing. I learned it later that North Korean used to carry out such plays to agitate and encourage boys and girls to raise their loyalty. That was the well-known propaganda techniques or brainwashing.

A few days passed and there was what appeared to be propaganda or news that said that the People's Army had been victorious and was approaching the Nakdong River, southeast corner of the peninsula of Korea. But when villagers were trying to check it out if it was true, the message or the slogan suddenly disappeared. It was only a month earlier, there was the announcement that said the liberation of South Korea was imminent, pasted on the front wall of the Consumer Association building. From mid-September 1950, wounded soldiers of the People's Army appeared in the villages and then moved to the further north later. The word "strategic retreat" by the People's Army began to emerge here and there. One day, when it was thought that the number of wounded soldiers coming from Oeum or power plants increased, some regular soldiers with guns, with no sign of injury, also were moving with wounded. It was obviously the retreating. The ranks of the People's Army, marching north on foot, were passing through the village in one continuous line with no interruption, and it was too many to count. In my house, I was always reminded of the message from the Korean People's Army that my brother would be coming home soon. Neighbors were worried about what the world would be like if the South Korean soldiers come to the village, with blunt expressions.

My brother is a defector from People's Army

It was not until early evening that my older brother came in quietly and hid somewhere in my house. As darkness fell on the thatched houses in this mountain village, I heard quiet knocking on the back door of my home several times. "Are you Gwangjun?" I heard my mother's cautious quiet voice, as she sounded as though she was waiting for me in the late afternoon but much quieter this time. At that very moment I also heard what sounded was my brother's very quiet voices, but I could tell he was one who was saying "be quiet!"

As my brother entered through the back door that was left open, his haggard appearance appeared in the darkness and there were clear indications that he was exhausted, and he did not have much on his body, indicating he had lost a lot of things. His usual manly brave mien and physique was nowhere to be seen. My mother, who was always anxious and worried about us, said "after you were called up to the People's Army and sent to the front, I believed that you might be fighting in combat or whatever you do for what they force you to, but you will be alive somewhere. Oh yes! That was what I have believed." She did not cry. It was obvious motherly self-assurance. My brother later said that he was hiding in the mountains as a retreating soldier but still in the uniform of the North Korean People's Army. He moved only when it was dark. He was hungry. The glare from the outside was even scarier still.

The five houses in the section of the neighborhood, located at the foot of the mountain, separated by a hundred meters from the Min village, were facing each other and separated by the wooden fence between the attached houses. If something happened to one house, all five of them would know within a few moments. Even if no one asked or suggested, as if they had known it was as though it was their obligation, they let everyone know what is taking place if anything unusual would take place. Message spread very fast, sometime even that of some innocuous rumors too.

My grandmother and my mother greeted my brother quietly and looked at him as he was gulping the cooked rice with water. He just did not pay any attention to anyone in the room. There was not a light in the house, but he was able to finish the meal.

Although it is not easy to trace the dates one lived through the war, it was estimated to be a few days past mid-October. It was about an hour after sunset, and as it was in the mountainous area of Gangwon-do, the temperature dropped faster, and it was already very cold. During the day, the soldiers of the People's Army, falling behind the main group, were hiding in the wood of the mountains. They passed through the villages at night and were heading north along the road. It is a countryside, quite remote from any urban town, and so it might have taken another day for the South Korean forces to arrive in the village area. South Korean troops were stationed in the village of Hwacheon-eup, and the messages with no clear source but it was a rumor from the neighboring Hwacheon-eup that Cheorlwon and Geumhwa were already being invaded by the allied forces.

Just two days earlier, the People's Army was encouraging the villagers to evacuate the village and move to the north, advising "we must protect the peoples north of the 38th parallel because they are our peoples." Also, they urged villagers to take the evacuation route to the north, saying that the invading South Korean army were merciless, and they would just kill anyone randomly. The People's Army soldier might have been naïve and ignorant about the fact that the villagers would not easily abandon their old hometown. The villager might have hesitated for a moment or two as they knew the red army kept urging to abandon their home, but at the end, the villagers moved pretending to evacuate the village and secretly entered wooded mountains nearby at night, digging the ground like an air-raid shelter, not too far from the village. They hid themselves there until a chance to move arrived. Fortunately, there have been rumors that the chairman of the People's Committee, who appeared in front of the town with a makeshift paper horn earlier in the morning to speak, but he must have decided not to speak and left the town earlier.

However, the perception of some South Korean residents here in Pungsan-ri after the end of the war were not what it used to be. On the day of the war started in June 1950, many men dressed as supply crews went to Chuncheon, South Korea. Those men came back after having seen the way of life of ordinary South Koreans. By what they saw, they were surprised by the life of southerners comparing to what he remembered about the life in the north. The kitchen utensils they brought from an vacant house left by the south Korean owners looked like that belong to the house of the wealthy households of the North Korea. The rumors spread by the North Korean officials in the village were that South Koreans were so oppressed that they were virtually naked and starved, until then.

The children of the village began to pay attention to what the grown-ups were talking about. It was as if Pungsan-ri, my hometown, was at some sort of a turning point for a big change. In Pyeongchon, if there was a decent man who could carry heavy loads, he should have escaped to the north already or just hid somewhere in the mountains. If they did not, they should have faced South Korean soldiers very next day. The People's Army was retreating hurriedly, and the South Korean Army was pursuing them from some distance, but a clear front line was not formed yet. I heard gunshots from time to time, but even that was all left and the village became totally quiet.

The older brother of a friend of mine took his turn to say that he was a sergeant in the People's Army and was assigned to build a bridge. So, if the main supply route across the river were cut off a temporary bridge had to be built. He took the responsibility to build a temporary bridge in such cases. But he left his unit of the North Korean Army while it was retreating to north. No doubt, he became a fugitive or a traitor, in the eyes of the northerners. He could not go any further to the north as he certainly could not imagine he would leave all his family behind, not to mention his mother. He knew well that all his family depended on him, above all else. He knew all well that the further north he went, the further he would be away from his family. Furthermore, he was not likely to be able to see his family again if he left them, then. He was 17-year-old then and he was an ordinary young man of countryside, and naïve he was. His younger brother, the friend of mine, must be in deep grief over the predicament of what his older brother had to face for his future and simply wished he did have enough time to be together. He was initially deployed in one of the battles in Gangwon-do province, and as the retreat of the North Korean People's Army began, he left the ranks surreptitiously when the troop was passing through Hwacheon and approaching Cheolwon. I cannot imagine what must have gone through in his mind as he was passing through the familiar geography. He walked along the road that was extending to the southeast and some by the road entering the mountains. A couple of days passed, and this brother of my friend found some refugees hiding in the wood. It was not too difficult to start a conversation with them. He asked some refugees where they were. They said it was Hwacheon-myeon, quite certainly. He did not talk for a long time before he started to calculate a plan in his mind. He decided to check more about the area he was in. With some hesitancy, he asked them if they knew the family by the name so and so, which was his parents' names. He was trying to check if they knew some folks in his village or even his home. When he spoke again, he tried to reassure them that he was safe to deal with. By then he was assuring himself that if the soldiers from the south arrived in the area in that moment, he would turn himself in to surrender without any hesitation. He knew well that he was one who had to make all the decision soon or later after careful calculation. He realized very well that there was no family member who could help him.

My Brother was a South Korean Security Guard

The next day, a truck carrying South Korean soldiers crashed some structure in the village. The sound was like a huge storm in a quiet village. The arrival of South Korean troops was expected. A military truck carrying dozens of soldiers appeared in Pungsan-ri. The new road, built by the North Korean soldiers in preparation of the war strategically, ended up being used by the South Korean army vehicles first time, ironically. The soldiers who got off the truck in the front yard of the public hall shouted toward the houses around; "everyone will be safe. Please get out of the house!" A little while past and then several men and women started to appear on the street. The soldiers spoke to them that they knew the difficulties the villagers went through, and they should discuss the matter to lead a normal life with peace of mind. At my home, one of the family insisted that my older brother should not go out to the street alone yet. When he had to, my mother would accompany him. Finally, we decided to watch from the front of the house, and otherwise the family would use a smaller private door in the back.

But what was it? Next day, two soldiers from the south holding rifles were there in front of the main door as though they were waiting for us. They moved toward us as soon as we opened the door. They called our name, "Im Kwang-Jun?" We could not help but to be shocked. We started to tremble. Unbeknown to us, the older brother of mine was already walking with his hand raised high, a gesture of surrender. He was still in the uniform of the North Korean People's Army which had all the markings of North Korean soldier, such as epaulets, though they were removed. One of the South Korean soldiers searched his body. And then, the soldiers smiled and said, "You're a lucky guy. You'll be fine. Get in the car. You just must do what you are told, and then you will be fine." The soldier gestured to take the lead. His tone was a bit stiff, but he gave me some reassurance and peace of mind.

After my brother was taken away by the soldier of the south, my family and I were wandering about his whereabouts, and we couldn't figure out what took place earlier on the street of the village. First, some grownups started guessing that my brother would not be punished, judging by the kindness and the kind reassuring words of the soldiers who took him away. The most serious question of mine was that even though he hid the fact that he was hiding in the house, how anyone other than my family knew about it, and furthermore why the South Korean soldier treat him so gently and kindly? I wished someone could explain why. This question was in fact answered three days after my brother was taken away. The message said that that if we wished to see my brother, visit the Hwacheon Police Station in town, and then we would be allowed to see him. The message also said that the South Korean government was taking measures so that those who was sincere and innocent and who surrendered like my brother could be hired as security agents for the South Korean Authority. In fact, it was a back door rumor that there was even a briefing session was taking place explaining what the security officers were doing in the town already. I then heard that someone saw my brother was working as a security guard in town already. Someone even said that he approached a villager who came to the market in town asking about my family also. My mother was assured and was happy that her son had been freed from any extreme situation and now allowed to live nearby, not too far from home. In late autumn, we, the family, wished that the older brother would be well and was leading life with good aspirations and prayers.

Rural areas were Lawless

Pyeongchon was a village of the largest number of households in Pungsan-ri, with about 50 households. The village suffered an unprecedented and terrifying plague during the war and the entire villagers were exhausted. A rumor said that two families had contracted the infectious disease and another story was that in one family all five members were infected and ill. Among them, an elderly person who had just passed the sixty years of age died first within ten days of infection. As it was the first such a terrifying epidemic that attacked the village and it had never been heard in Pungsan-ri until then. It is undeniably the most major calamity this village ever experienced.

Some households could not find anyone who could work for the farms for the season and could not even harvest in the fall. They were just going to have to face the winter without any crops being harvested. In Pyeongchon, some villagers with better circumstances either fled to the north after the early harvest was over or already took refuge in the mountains. So, it was difficult to find even female workers for the harvesting. On top of that, men were conscripted into the army from the age of 17, and those who were conscripted at the age 50 became supply crews for the People's Army. Those who came back from the compulsory workers for either side during the harsh war, if he didn't run away before the end of the war, whichever side you might have been ended up with, it became obvious that one is likely to be sacrificed one way or another. If he didn't die, he would be in a situation where he had to endure the hard life with the rest of the people in his hometown while being hit here and there by the forces of either side.

During the war, bombs destroyed many houses in my village. Only 30 houses escaped from destruction. Those houses were also difficult to access during the day because of the ever-watchful allied bombers and the frequent appearance of the fighter jet and their air strikes. I learned later that the bombings by the fighters or bombers on the north of the 38th parallel were indiscriminate and heavy. For this reason, North Koreans had to go to their home after sunset and leave their homes early in the morning before dawn to hide deep in the wooded hills or deep in the mountains. On top of that, it was difficult to predict a day ahead for anyone as anything could happen and even because of random spreading of such infectious disease, causing severe diarrhea leading into severe dehydration and that might lead into serious malaise such as seizures. Some people even raise their wall, as though they could protect themselves from such illness spreading in their neighbors as though raising the walls of their hearts.

Then, there were rumors arriving from places time to time. The front line of the war suddenly moved quickly to the south as the People's Army, which was busily retreating to the north not so long ago, suddenly turned around and strangely started counterattacking the south, by the late autumn. A month earlier, it was said that the South Korean army advancing to the north was reaching near the Yalu River. The South Korean and the allied forces advancing north suddenly met with the brick wall by sudden appearance of the Chinese communist forces, obviously to support North Korean. In fact, it is said that the front line was moving to the south very fast since the Chinese forces were massive and many time more than the north Korean. Some news said it was more than a million. It was a sheer human wave. We thought it would take several more days or weeks before the newly advancing Northern forces to reach Hwacheon. But then, also the rumors circulated that the People's Army had already arrived and hid in the mountains in Pungsan-ri area. They were poised to come down to the village at any time. The authenticity of such rumors was not confirmed, and yet in the villages like Pungsan-ri, the vacuum of military forces kept the village calm for a month or so, causing eerie sense and scary uncertainty for some time. Meanwhile, during the day times, the allied fighter planes made flight and attacked two or three times a day with those scary machine gun sounds. In between these flights the whole place, the village, the fields, and the mountains were calm and quiet, in fact at times too quiet to be ghostly. A few days of quietude might have passed, but if what looked like a man, just a figure, not necessarily a real man or soldier in the visible field from the sky, the fighter planes appeared from nowhere and would attack the figure with machine guns mercilessly. When the villagers were running out of food, some folks of the Pyeongchon would go down to the field at night, to avoid the planes, and even they thresh the rice at night by modifying the threshing grounds and schedule. Ironically, but happily, the farmers would take the sigh of relief that year, as they wouldn't be visited by tax inspectors in that year; ordinarily he should have visited the farms during the harvest season, around this time of the year. But this year none will show up because of the war. The in-kind tax paid for the crops produced by the farming was determined by measuring the amount of the rice bran after the threshing of crops, after the harvest.

In my home, since my brother left home and because of the outbreak of the epidemic, no one could move or even evacuate the house, and it scared us. It appeared that some families had gone northward, in groups of five or six families. Right behind my home was the home of a friend of mine in the same class as mine at school. All the homes were not well kept in shape as there was none who could care for the house because the head of the household was taken away to work in the unit of the North Korean military. It was not too long since the house lost head of the household, and the shape of the houses showed as though it had been a very long time since the house was left vacant.

Thousands of her neighbors, who had seen their neighbors leaving one by one, were muttering like they all should have left too. My family, who probably could not vacate the house and became only family, end up remaining in the home of their own. This was the only household that came to the People's Army Unit office governing the village. This was the only household that decided to stay in the village and came to ask for rice, saying they would rather eat and remain in the village than go somewhere they do not know and starve. If the South Korean army occupied the village, they would have made the same request and the response by them might have been the same.

About 70% of the people of Pungsan-ri fled to the north. Still, the people remaining in the Pungsan-ri were trying to trust the northern army because of their ardent persuasion that Northern Military said that if the South Korean army entered the village, there would be merciless killing by them. Unlike the big cities, rural residents experienced the kindness of South Korean soldiers though it was only very short period during their northward march, but since the times they contacted and lived their lives by listening to the North Korean Communist Party's education and propaganda much longer, they had not been able to know or trust the South Korean military and what they really could do for them as they did not use such constant propaganda like the North Korean Military. One thing was certain, however, that the perception by the uneducated farmers and newly educated school children was very different, that is the grownup was different from the children who were educated. The grown-ups were reluctant to speak out openly which side was good and/or which side was bad.

My Brother was A Second Gunner

There was a rumor that the North Korean army was coming back, and it became true. One day, the chilly day of the early winter, my older brother opened the back door of the house and entered in the same shape as before, taking advantage of the darkness of the moonless night, as if he had promised before. He again left the ranks of the South Korean security forces which was withdrawing to the south as the North Korean troop was pushing south in the winter. He looked restless, pacing in the room as if he was looking for something, some solution as though he was in a deep dilemma.

He called my mother, who was about to go to the place where my father was staying, but she asked him about the situation of the village. He said he was hurrying about what to do. The story he revealed was that the remnants of the People's Army were already forming their ranks in the northern mountainous area, the South Korean Army had been already ordered to withdraw, and the South Korean security personnel whom my maternal uncle used to work for left for the south already. He could not imagine and he would go to the south alone, leaving his older brother behind. Also, there was nothing I could say to my brother on Mother's Day, who believed my home was the safest place. No matter how much the world changed, we lived in that slanted thatched house. I didn't know which one world well and which people were right. They are all ignorant, so when they are sad or lonely, they only crawl into the family bosom.

All night long, the family discussed how they could escape the village to get away from the problem. But my older brother, knowing that he could not leave his family in this home behind, was calculating and imagining ways as a reasonable solution. He must have felt like he was losing his mind as he imagined that the chances of his survival at the time were only a half and half of what should have been. Then, he changed his mind again and decided the best solution was that he should run away. However, he just could not make up his mind. He kept back and forth again and again. But whatever his brother's decision might have been it looked either good or bad. The sadness of leaving his mother and family behind and the fear of being caught and getting death sentence were constantly intruding in one's head. My brother must have prepared in his mind resolutely that he might be tortured, executed, or indescribably suffering if he was caught by the Northern Korean People's Army. To the defector of the People's Army worked such as a security guard for the South Korean side, it certainly would be judged as a crime of treason. One cannot imagine what kind of punishment would be imposed. We all felt helpless. All the family were downcast only staring at the floor, as if everyone must have been thinking they were hanging on the edge of a cliff.

At last, a little late in the morning, several North Korean soldiers appeared in town. Two soldiers from the group started surveying the village, checking the houses one by one. One of them went in and out of the private gate of a house that was located on the outskirts of the village. When an old woman saw one of the North Korean soldiers holding his gun high as if he was aiming at something, she approached the soldier and begged. "Please don't! We have a child in the house." she begged. It sounded like she was saying 'save me,' as she was muttering as she was also frightened as though the gun of one soldier was pointed at her. Then, one of the soldiers standing behind a pole near a house shouted toward the room of the house. "Raise all your weapons high and come out." Although his brother had no weapons, the soldier was quite agile in dealing with any suspect or enemy. He must have been taught very well or experienced. My brother raised his hand in the gesture of surrendering and walked out of the room. The soldier shouted at my brother; "Hey you! Get down flat!" slamming my brother's shoulder with the rifle buttstock. While my brother fell on his face, uttering "Hey!", the soldier stepped in the room which my brother was in a few minutes earlier. Finding out there was no weapon, the room was empty, the soldier shouted at my brother again questioning something.

At this moment, the soldier standing outside of the house sent a signal toward the public hall, shouting "stay there a minute." He then summoned the other soldiers who were inside the house as if something urgent needed to be taken care of. And then he walked away. The People's Army headquarters was set up in the public hall of the town. Two soldiers came from there and dragged my brother away.

About midday, the messenger from the People's Army came to the village. He announced with a low tone of voice 'You will be shot as a traitor. Don't approach the scene.' Although the tone was particularly soft the announcement was frightening. All the families soon started weeping and wailing. The place became the ocean of tears. As expected, we were helpless, and that was all we could expect and there was no more helpful idea under the circumstance. It was completely hopeless. My mother, who followed him on the road from her house, weeping and dropping her tear on the cold bare ground. I had to take her duvet and wrap me and my mother. My grandmother walked into her room first with her sister, who gestured to me to help my mother to the room. No one approached our house by then and the place became deadly quiet.

During the night, the intermittent sound of gunshots was heard. The sound of gunshots seemed to be coming from the power plant, about 30 miles away. The loud sounds of gunshots came on repeatedly for a few minutes. It then became quiet for some time as though they were entering a state of order. The long silence lasted for several hours. It appeared that my grandmother and my mother were worried about how to collect the body of their child. My mother kept silent for a long time. She was up all night in tears, and the grandmother stood in front of the private gate of the house early in the morning. It was certain that she was hoping for any message about her grandson might come. She stared at the public hall motionlessly. The building was a couple of hundred meters in distance. At last, she called me and pointed, with her finger, to a soldier in a People's Army uniform. He was staggering toward them. Alas, it was her son, the older son. He beckoned to me before even coming closer. He gestured as though he wanted to grab me. I approached him quickly and grabbed him. He was barely able to walk now. I could not help but burst into tears. This my older brother said "you shouldn't cry" in a tired and whispering voice. I could barely hear him. My brother was almost on the verge of collapse. I know what the interrogation by the Red Army was like. Not only I have been beaten many times, but also, I have been subjected to various kinds of tortures when they interrogate me whatever information they wanted to squeeze out of me. It was said that, in danger of being shot, the officers often gave the order to stop the torture and they sent the victims to the front line. The fighting around the power plant was unfavorable for the People's Army side as they were short of the men, and they could not help but being the targets by the allied forces.

There was nothing much the family could offer other than let my brother sleep. But before he could rest enough, during the night, my brother and we were together only for a brief period, and he had to leave us to report to the headquarters of the People's Army in the public hall early that morning. A long gun was already hung from his brother's drooped shoulder.

In the south, about 15-ri (35 miles) away from the town, apparently fierce fighting was taking place. The roars of the cannon firing from Hwacheon Power Plant was heard. My brother now held a rifle, but it was nothing but to put into use as a bullet holder. We had very little doubt that he was in fact dragged away by the People's Army soldiers to the place for his execution.

Confession

The road into the valley was wet after the sprinkle. The grass covered by the raindrops was stepped on by the feet and it offended my heart for some reason. The innocent and indifferent grass along the roadside flourished even during the war. Occasional sounds of cannons and gunshots coming from afar were heard, otherwise there was silence in the misty valley. I had visited the village of Sojukgol several times with my grandmother and my mother before the war. They used to work in the fields of the Sojukgol. But now everything has changed.

I did not know who it was, but I heard several soldiers were shot in the barracks of the People's Army. I was on my way to check out if my brother was one of them. My mother was rushing to the barracks too, from time to time halting to catch her breath and then resuming her running and fast walk, again. 'You must stay alive somewhere, you cannot leave me laying here?' She was trying to calm her spirit, but she could not hold back her tears and she was reciting those words again and again. She was keeping her distance from her mother, who was walking a few steps ahead of her. Still, not knowing what was going to happen soon, she then took a deep breath and slowed down her pace.

Suddenly, the image of my brother's face, in moaning with pain having been beaten with rifle by a soldier of the People's Army, came to my mind. The pain was harsh in my heart. My grandmother was several steps ahead of my mother, staring through her cowl. She murmured something and then she moved on to her again. My mother then found that my grandmother was moving fast, and a sickle was in her hand. It reminded me that a People's Army officer who said that she, his grandmother, should be used as a bullet proof jacket, during the fighting near the power plant. It made his mother's heart sink. I could not stop my tears as I was following my mother and my grandmother. My mother said, "you must not follow me." Suddenly, I had deep sorrow that I felt so sorry for my brother. My mother and my grandmother looked so helpless, but I could not help them. I was so despondent that I just wished to flop down and cry at the top of my lung 'Mother!' in the Gangwon dialect. Grandmother speeded up a little. She reached the building and stepped into the backyard of the building. She looked for the body of her grandson. She must have thought that she should scour the corpses with a scythe. She did not find the body of her grandson whom she assumed dead.

My grandmother left the place a little while later, and she then called me. It seems that the grandmother told my mother not to follow her. But I was already following her. She soon noticed. My grandmother waved and signaled my mother to go down the valley. There were seven corpses, but none was that of my brother. I noticed the sound of some relief in my mother's voice.

It was in the middle of winter, but when I took a step off the road there was sleet which was covered with rain just fell. It seemed that the winter was warmer for some time, this time of the year. My mother and I were walking without a word. Still, I was occupied with the fierce fight around the powerplant that had been pushed and pulled with attacking each side for days. Had my older brother been able to survive the battlefield, could he have just passed by his house on the way back to the north? When we reached the thought like that, we could not help but feel very sad.

My mother, who had a hard time taking care of my grandmother when she was sick and stayed in bed, also succumbed to the hardship, and ended up lying down herself. Though the grandmother did not say it, she was carrying her sick body for the past several days. Even though I thought that the disease in my family has been like the plague that everyone is afraid of. There was no point checking it out, but one can guess easily. Even if they knew what the disease was, what could they do? Typhoid like intestinal infections were commonplace then. The prevention was very difficult, and people then thought the illness certainly would kill the victim at last as there was no cure or any medicine that can even ease the condition. The Typhoid was death knell, then.

It was said that the number of people suffering from the infectious diseases in the neighborhood is already rising, and on some days the death toll exceeds two or three a day. Now, I hear the news in the neighborhood all the time; they talk about the disease when they greet each other, the sound of laud greeting over the fences in all about the disease, and constant message about who became the next victims and so forth.

But it seemed that the several unfortunate happenings came at the same time all at once. As if they were all interconnected, a problem arose in one place and then several problems followed. It was winter, so there was urgent need for firewood as the house with the plague had to keep the room with the patient should be warmer. Collecting the needed firewood was the most urgent, but very hard. A few oak trees were standing along the mountain road. It was the road I used to climb up to the mountain. It was in the shade and the snow piled up on the trunks. It was not so difficult to cut down the young branches of the oak as they only grew the height of a thatched house. I had to make a fire in the kitchen quickly that would warm the floor of the room. I slashed the branch of the wood I have collected with the tip of the scythe. I hit one of the wood the wrong way and ended up cutting the shin of my left leg. Blood flowed immediately. But I could not do anything about the wound although I was in severe pain. I tried to stop the bleeding by pressing the wound with my pants. Earlier, the man of the village who was known to be arrogant and pretentious, came by the tree where I was injured. He was the chairman of the village people's committee. "If you cut down trees, you will be punished. You should have known that. Come down from the tree quickly." The man went away without another word, I could not tell whether he was busy or meant to look busy.

The day my mother passed away

The light could not be turned on properly. My grandmother and my mother were skipping meals in the cold. Those grown-ups were all silent as though they were in a house of grieving. I could not appreciate what that was all about. I had the feeling that it was now my responsibility for whatever I had to do. First, what I had to do was to take my younger brother to the foot of the mountain and we had to pick up firewood. My younger brother was only 3 years old, and I was approaching 12 years of age.

I tried several times to bring some porridge of the hulled millet on the spoon to her mouth, the porridge that I made the night before, but it was in vain. I swore to watch my mother by staying in the room and right at her bed side, but sometimes when my sister fell asleep, I end up falling asleep too. When she woke up screaming as though she was awakened by nightmare or something, my grandmother would sit up and mutter in an angry voice. By then my mother was sitting up in the corner of her room already. And yet, she was not moving. There is no answer even when I call "Mother! Mother!". She sat down there, and she breathed. "Mom!... I was wrong. I…" I could not help but cry and whatever I said she did not respond. She now could not even sit straight. She seemed to try to say something. I wondered. What did she want to say? It sounded like she was mumbling though out her lifetime, she was a child to her mother who lacked what she should have and was in deep remorse. Even if my grandmother did not know what she was saying, her thought was that she must be mourning the death of her child. She mumbled pointing to her daughter-in-law 'can she leave her children and us, leave first?'

Waiting for the dawn, I announced my mother's death, and I let my maternal grandmother's family upstairs know, too. With the help of my grand aunt the younger sister of my grandmother, and her mother eventually buried my mother's body in the head of the field. Sitting by the shabby tomb, I wailed aloud as if calling my mother to come alive. "Son, go home now." I was hanging around next to my mother's body until I heard the voice of an old woman who lived in a secluded house at the foot of the mountain.

Helping the Chinese Military to Cook

The sound of shells, flying from the nearby power plant and falling outside Dong-gu, Pyeongchon, was so loud and then followed by sudden eerie silence. As the sun went down behind the hill, soldiers of about 80 men were passing by the road near the village, chattering casually. It sounded like no Korean. It was the Chinese. The army, estimated to be several dozen, seemed to be preparing the formation for the upcoming battle The half of it was lining up the main road and the other half by the mountain road. By the Chinese Communist Forces moving in the village in a hustle and bustle, I could tell that the battle must be taking place farther south of Pungsan-ri.

My maternal grandmother, who seemed to have recovered some strength, said, 'we should go into the mountains,' and packed a pile of blankets and a small sack of rice. The grandmother, who was still not quite well, took her two grandsons and moved into the vacant shelter in Yokgol. In the evening, she continued to keep a pit of fire with the dry tree branches. The fire pit seemed perfect for cooking rice or warming us to forget the cold air. She was showing her grandmotherly earnestness that she had to fight the plague and get up. She didn't skip the meals, although she had a hard time eating more than a few spoonful's porridge. As if she was aware of this situation, her younger sister, the younger grandaunt sent her daughter-in-law, who was alone, to our shelter. To me this woman was a distant aunt, but she said she had come to look after her eldest among the relatives. This grandaunt's son was also drafted into the military. She had no idea whereabout of her daughter-in-law but stays in her mind always. That may have something to do with her thoughtful helping this relative.

During such a predicament, one day, fierce battles and lulls were repeated alternatingly, in front of the air-raid shelter we were in, we heard the voice of a person we didn't know what it meant. Immediately, we held our breath at the thought that they might be the Chinese Army. Then, after the sound of 'clicking' and loading bullets in the guns, the gunfire sounded and appeared to be bullets were entering the shelter. The grandaunt patted me on my shoulder and gesturing go out by her chin. When I reached out and waved one hand, I waved my hand instead of the muzzle, signaling everyone to come out. The Chinese soldier didn't even think about checking inside of the shelter anymore, and only waved us to follow him. The valley was wider near the field. We saw a dozen of Chinese soldiers stood lining obliquely. The postures were for the readiness for a battle.

One of the soldiers asked where the people were, in a Korean that was like stuttering but understandable. He ordered us to follow them as they lead for their advance. The Chinese soldier handed us a handful of dried hard cookies. Not knowing what their intentions were, I nonchalantly walked into the town. Upon reaching the entrance to Sangpyeong Village, the first good house that appeared was my mother's cousin's house. The Chinese soldier sounded like he was saying, 'people, you go home,' in Korean.

The Chinese Communist Army Company Headquarters was set up in this house they reached. From the first day I met them, I helped them by cooking and taking care of the fire in the furnace. I then ate and ate. It was my first time trying this much food, but it was delicious as I was so hungry. On that first day arriving, all the Chinese, except for the sentries, seemed to have gone to the bed early. I slept in a pile of straw on the rice paddy field in front of the house. I must have fallen into a deep sleep. When I woke up to the sudden low-flying sound of a reconnaissance plane, the sun was already hanging over the mountain. With the sun rise, the entire army of the company sang the military songs repeatedly like a campaign ceremony. I couldn't figure out what the songs meant, but I heard that what I still remember is 'Meyu Gongzantang, Meyu-changong'. The soldier, a cook at the headquarters, sang more and more as though he was trying to teach me the song while I was helping him tidy things up in the place for him. Suddenly, an allied plane flew over in low flying. The Chinese soldiers, who were preparing for the campaign, immediately stopped singing and ran to the foot of the mountain with other soldiers. The plane bombed a few minutes later hitting some empty road of the farm.

The company troops, that had just left for the direction of the power plant and the place, was replaced with local troops. It seemed that they would soon engage in a battle. With a gun stood at the entrance of the kitchen, the cook showed me a castor bean leaf and pointed to the mountain, trying to tell me to go up to the hill and look for something like that. Luckily, at the foot of the mountain, about 200 meters away from the compound, the castor bean plots were scattered like outdated corn plots. The cook seemed to already know where the castor beans were. The cook seemed to accept the leaves I brought, he seemed to like my collection, and he even thanked me for the dried leaves.

In the large cauldron in the kitchen, some soybean oil and buckwheat flour were always boiled. Adding some greens and something that looks like soy sauce to adjust the seasoning, it was boiled continuously, and it became a porridge ready to be eaten. Even before leaving for the battlefield, the soldiers could be seen hanging around the kitchen and eating this porridge in the metal cup that was usually hung on their belt.

The cook, who was waiting for the hungry troops to arrive, gave me a bowl of porridge and pointed to a straw bale standing in the paddy field, motioning I should be somewhere else to eat the food. He must have heard from somewhere that it would be better to hide and eat, as though it was a sort of dictum.

I walked and passed the front of a house, but I didn't want to go into it. I was standing behind the pile of straw bales near the grain field and started to eat my porridge. I happened to glance the direction of Yokgol in the distance. Just at that moment, I saw a person was coming from the valley. 'Awe, Grandma'. Almost came out of my mouth. Only then, I was reminded about my family in the bomb shelter. It was my aunt who was approaching. Yes, it was her. His aunt was waving her hand as a signal to someone gesturing to move faster. Who was she waving to? What happened? I then realized that I had forgotten everything about my family all this time. In that moment, my grandmother's face was floating in mind. It made me sad instantly. My grandmother, the last grown-up, the oldest who looked after us came into my heart right away. She must have passed away. My aunt used to run fast, but her tears were covering her face and her feet were in walking pace. As she made her way across the paddy fields to the valley and my aunt lay my grandmother down, she said "Your grandmother is dead." As I was about to overtake the weight, she said, 'I need to tell my younger grandmother myself'. Yes, it was what I was going to do. But then, I also realized that there was no one else to tell.

My grandmother was a kind person. She would not allow us to be paid for a single spoonful she offered even if she was the one who cooked the meal and prepared the whole table. Also, at the family table she would encourage everyone to be sure that my brothers start to eat before anyone else eats. It was expected, but it shocked me as much as my mother when it was seen in the very beginning. It may be because she cared for her grandchildren, but it was because my grandmother was the only adult who took care of and worried about us brothers until the very end, better than anyone else.

My aunt told me to stay with my brother, and she said, "Don't come back to follow me" and then she added "From now on, you have to live with your grandmother." She turned around. I thought it was odd, and I carried my brother down the valley, looking towards the side of the shelter. My aunt was already climbing the ridge towards the passage to go somewhere else; I did not know where. She was married in Pungsan-ri. But I did not know where she was heading. Even during war, she wanted to leave Yokgol to find a place where she could accept the place, she could settle down herself and live with.

Begging for forgiveness

I was carrying her younger brother on the way to the home of my younger grandmother to convey the message about the death of her sister. I came across the same road that I went through when my mother passed away. My maternal grandmother, who lost her husband shortly after her marriage, was allowed to stay in the little house belonging to her younger brother. She was then pregnant with my mother. It must have been following the custom at that time. To me, it was always called 'the little maternal grandmother's house'.

It was at this time that I realized that my footsteps would be on the road of aimless wandering after the news of my grandmother's death was announced in her home. Looking back now, during the Korean War, often families were broken; the parents and the children were separated, and they were scattered. Then, they went through the agonizing hardship. There was hopelessly very little way to make a living after escaping from the war with bare hands. Who should be blamed? There are no other ways to say anything other than the expression, "I wonder if everyone was terrified."

A few days earlier, one of my uncles, my mother's younger brother, Gwang-yi, began to whimper with sickness. He could not eat, and he had fever. It must have been an infectious disease. Then, my younger brother, who had voracious appetite began to lose his appetite and became thin after losing weight for a short period. I started feeling sick too, and I also started losing volition for anything. Even if I might be hungry, I had no desire to cook for myself. Even some well-prepared food may be left untouched for several days, whether it is porridge or rice. But somehow, we all seemed to be able to endure for a while. One day, I realized belatedly that the rice had run out. I searched for any food left in an air-raid shelter in the upper valley. When I went in and looked for anything to eat, I saw a large bowl of white rice and a sack full of something that looked edible. It was cooked to my eyes. As soon as I tried to scoop out the rice with a spoon, the pile of rice collapsed helplessly. Still, after seeing the rice, I ate a couple of spoonsful without hesitation. But somehow, I couldn't eat any more afterward. Was it rot? Although it appeared rotten, the rice had a white and bright appearance, but then it appears to be also easily blown away.

The battle seemed to continue without the battle line moving from the Hwacheon area. The frontline between the allied side, the UN forces, and the communist side with Chinese and North Korean forces, were not moving as it must have been in stalemate. There were even funny telltale stories. At one time, when the People's Army put their guns inside an air defense shelter and then accused themselves why they didn't evacuate(retreat) to the north, and then very next day the South Korean Army appeared in the same bunker and insisted that there was not a Northern soldier, and they did not know where the Korean People's Army was. We were living in the area where we had to leave quickly to survive, either to the north or to the south, sometime to both ways on same days. I learned later that the northern side, the area just outside of Hwacheon, was directly connected to the Iron Triangle, where the well recorded long and fierce battle was fought with tens of thousands of casualties on both sides for a long time, in the Korean War. But then the front-line facing opponent each other became quieter in the middle of June 1951 only with occasional scattered sounds of rifle or brief machine gun. It was obvious stale mate of the front line. But then the stalemate persisted for a long time.

It was a warm day in June 1951, it was relatively quieter other than occasional gun sound that was scattered and rare. We imagined that it was because of the spread of plague that had something to do with the quietude of the fighting front. We all felt very weak. My brother, who was able to walk well until a few days earlier, abruptly could not walk, not even crawl. I felt like I was losing my spirit too. I felt so helpless as not only I couldn't do anything about myself, but also for my brother, I just had to watch my younger brother helplessly although he was crying and crying. I did not know what to do for my brother. I started to feel fainty. I had a hard time resting well myself as I cannot find a way to be comfortable. I could not even sleep restfully. Sometimes, I didn't even know that I was sleeping or awakening, as I must be confused.

A day later my father appeared in the field near the entrance of the village. He came in a truck. The cargo was full of dried pollack. I wiped my eyes. It was like a dream to see my father and the load of the truck. It was not a dream; I was sure it was real. My father got out of the car and stood there with a big smile. It was much more than the amount stored in the Pungsan-ri Cooperative Association.

"Father!" I called him when I thought he was close enough I could hear my father's voice. I kept calling him. The valley was cleared and cleaned. Then, there was sound of a large gun shot as loud as a bomb was dropped deep in the valley and then the entire mountain sounded like it was shaking. The ground shook with the sound of three or four more shells falling in the field. With all sorts of cracking gun sounds following, I felt something was hitting my heart with the feeling that my heart was sinking. I turned my head and looked at the place where the dust was rising, and the pieces of rocks rolled down from the top of the hill. I thought I saw my father standing there with a truck loaded with something like drumsticks or dried fishes, but next moment I couldn't see my father any longer. At that moment, the ground nearby shook violently as the shells fell not too far from where I was. After that, a few more seconds of continuous small gun sound was heard, then the sounds of shell flying were heard, and next the sounds of the bombs hitting the ground with huge roars was heard whole area.

I was not hurt as I was lying on my stomach while I could hear the countless shells passing by and the loud sounds of the guns. I lay down next to a large pit that was created by the bombs and by the cannonballs. Meanwhile, I felt so sad as I was thinking that my father could not figure out where I was by all the rackets. Then, I fell asleep again.

I don't know how long I slept. It was very cold. At the foot of the mountain, there was an abandoned house, half of it looked destroyed. From one of the rooms without a wall on one side, one could see the sky. I stepped into the room and settled on a corner. I had no other thoughts but the feeling of sorrow about my father's demise. He wondered if he was dreaming about the whole thing, including seeing his father. Was it a so-called daydream? While I was preoccupied about the dream or dream like experience, I completely forgot my four-year-old brother, but then there I fell into a deep sleep again. I slept for a while and when I woke up it was early in the morning. It was very cold.

For a moment, somehow, I thought that my brother was somewhere alone.

'In the dark night, in the valley, my little one…'

I climbed up the mountain by the shadowy and gloomy valley at dawn. I called my younger brother by his name repeatedly in my sobbing voice for quite some time. 'Gwangsun! Gwangsun!' No, the event that marked the indelible end of my life was taking place. "Dear my brother, please keep alive!" The little one died in the shelter during the night. I thought the air from his nostrils was still warm, but that might have been my wishful thinking. There was no breath. I ripped open the blanket as though I was supplying enough air for him, and then rolled up his body with the blanket again, leaving only a small hole.

"Mom!" I was wondering if someone could tell me what this was all about. 'I killed my brother. Uh… I killed my own brother. What are you going to say about it?" I then cried aloud. "How can I be so indifferent and heartless? How could I let such a thing happen?"

Looking at my dead brother's face, I was terrified. My hand shook when I held my brother last time. I was frightened. I laid the body on the pile of dirt behind the bomb shelter. 'My dear brother! I was not good to you. Oh, my dear brother! Forgive me!' I trudge away from my brother's body. My steps became faster, and I was already about 10 meters away from him, then my speed was like I was running away. I was mumbling and saying like a chanting; 'forgive me, forgive me, my dear brother!' In the distance, in the village, I heard what appeared to be South Korean soldiers with guns on their shoulder speaking in loud voices. It was that the soldiers were encouraging the town people to come out from hiding with assuring tone of the voices. The soldiers were speaking in loud shouting voices at people to come out of the shelters or from hiding and telling them to come down the valley quickly. Since I left the body of my brother at the entrance of the destroyed bomb shelter these soldiers could find it easily, I thought. I was scared! I ran down to the village as fast as I could.

Even though I am over 80 years of my age, I still cry whenever I think about him as though I failed to look for my little brother then or as though I failed to keep him alive. I do the vein gesture of nudges as sort of an excuse or begging forgiveness. I could not help but to let his demise take place and I should have been able forget and erase it from my memory while I carried my life with hard and diligent working, but the memory is persistently coming back, more so now as I get older, with sorrow. Is it because of my nature to regret endlessly after committing any wrongdoing? Even if I start to have illness with symptoms of forgetfulness in my late age, will I still be forced to have such painful memories or suffer a sad daydream? Am I going to suffer the pain by the indelible memory that I blame myself for the loss of my baby brother?

In front of the Hapyeong Village Public Hall where, there was a commotion with several civilians near the two military trucks which were supposed to take us away from the town long time ago. As I think about it, I had to leave the place by the trucks which were sent for us specially. All that took place in my life and all the people I encountered in my life in that village until I had to leave came through in my mind like a panoramic sequence. Life in the small village of Pyeongchon, Pungsan-ri was enjoyable and entertaining when I was small. The small village now changed greatly and rapidly by the war. The changed village became a new world that the villagers had never seen before. The North Korean society was only criticized for their atrocities such as exploiting, oppressing, and so forth. That was more than the villagers could bear.

Some people already on those trucks appeared to be members of several households, and some were shouting for the trucks to wait until all the other members of the family to get on the truck. One man on the truck told me to get on another truck and threw a small sack of rice to the ground belong to me. It was a thoughtful gesture in such a chaotic situation. I felt grateful. It was the first time I saw him in the village, but he was showing such kindness that any grownup could show even during the war. It must have meant that it was understandable to see a child coming alone from a remote mountain valley during the war and trying to get on the truck to survive in a pathetic shape. It should provoke sympathy with concern how he could survive alone.

The driver of the truck, as soon as everyone there got on the truck, said he did not have much time to wait, and he started the vehicle. When I was the only one without a companion left on the cargo bay. He assured me that he would take me anywhere I could get a place to sleep. On the moving car, I was gradually losing my thought about my brother and what I had done in the valley while the truck was running in such speed. I was even forgetting something that I had done with my brother's body in the valley, a while ago. I was wondering with imagination if he wished me to forget about him as he was in a better place than I was. Or his spirit might be guiding me to forget what took place earlier and only thinking about getting out of the place to a safe place. So, I started to concentrate on where the best place might be I should go. When I got off the truck. I had to consider seriously where I should have chance to get food for my survival and where I should have stayed to sleep that was warm enough. I was still calculating about how to get any grains for meals, firwood to warm at night and cook the meals, and as such. The more I think about it, the more I became worried about my survival. This my new anxiety began to occupy me, and it persisted with a new preoccupation about new adventure in the new world that I had never been to in my life before. The only thought kept coming back was 'whatever I face I must deal with or fight for it."

I grabbed the small rice sack that contained a handful of rice with my both hands tightly lest I might lose.

Unforgettable memories of crossing the 38th parallel,

And the Korean War

Hie-Won Lee Hann

Two years before the Korean War started, my family just settled down in Inchon City in South Korea after two years' hardships in North Korea.

In Manchuria

Before our life started in North Korea, my family lived in Bongchon City (now called Shenyang) in Manchuria. My three sisters and I were all born in Shenyang. Approaching the end of the WWII, Manchuria was relentlessly showered by American air raids. We spent long hours in an underground shelter. As a child, I was anxious to see the bombing airplanes, and sneaked out to see how the planes looked like. Watching the bombs being dropped one after another from way up high by the smart looking silvery Boeing 29 of American bombers was some experience. The American bombers flew so high that the Japanese anti-aircraft machine guns were unable to reach them. Whenever we heard the remote but distinct sound of the Boeing-29, followed by a loud siren, we ran down to the underground shelter.

Crossing the Yalu and life in North Korea

After WWII ended on August 15, 1945, by the Japanese surrender, my family returned to my father's hometown, Namsi City in North Korea, joining to live with my paternal grandparents. For the next two years, we encountered multiple adversities under the North Korean communist regime. Father returned to Shenyang in Manchuria to help founding the ethnic school for the large number of Koreans who remained in the city. He later left Shenyang when Mao's army approached. My father and other Koreans went to Chunjin City, China, which was still under Chiang Kai-shek's control. My father subsequently was able to come to Inchon, South Korea on a navy landing ship (LST) with the help of the United States Navy.

Having spent with my grandparent in North Korea, my mother, my three sisters (ages 6-year-old, 3 year, and 3 months old) and I (9-year-old) had to join my father in South Korea. We said good-bye to my paternal grandparents and took a train to the south toward the 38th parallel. My mother planned to cross the 38th parallel at night with the help of a paid guide. In a house near the border, people with the same plan as ours filled the room waiting for the night. However, before dark, North Korean soldiers came in the house shouting and kicking the door, exposing all of us in the room. While all of us were forced out and had to form a line, my mother told me surreptitiously to throw away the South Korean paper money which I hid in my inside pockets. Making an excuse to relieve myself, I went up to a nearby hill and placed the South Korean money (a large sum) under a patch of small bean plant. What a pity to throw away such decent sums of the money my mother had so carefully saved! With two North Korean armed soldiers in front and back of us, we were forced to walk all night toward the nearby city, Haejoo, and at dawn we arrived at a house, once a rich merchant's mansion. Obviously, the house was purged and converted into a detention center.

Several attempted escapees who had been caught at the border filled every room. We were detained for a week. Each person underwent the interview for their attempted escape and was ordered back home to North Korea. When my mother returned after the interview, I expected that we would be sent back to the north, to my paternal grandparents' home perhaps. However, my mother, somewhat confused, said, "strange, he told me to go to South Korea." Before we could comprehend the situation, an officer in North Korean uniform but with kind speech and gestures came and asked us to get on his truck. We were puzzled and more anxious. The officer took us to the border at the 38th parallel and the riverbank was in ebb tide at that time. He told us to hurry to cross the border while the tide was in ebb. He pointed us towards South Korea, a faraway riverbank across with some trees. My mother with a 3-year-old on her back, I with my 3-month-old sister on my back, and my 6-year-old sister carrying a blanket, walked as fast as we could over the soft but solid floor of the riverbank exposed after the tide-out.

Crossing the 38th Parallel

As I recall, it was a blessing that we were arrested and detained, and then quite unexpectedly we were let go to cross the 38th parallel at daytime. It was quite an unexpected blessing. If we were not caught and tried to cross over the mountain at the border in the night, my family would have been impossible to keep up with the speed of the grown-ups in the group crossing the dangerous border guarded by the armed soldiers. If my 3-month-old sister had made any sound, that would have invited gunshots of the guards. Indeed, hundreds of people lost their lives while crossing the border at night, we were told.

Later, we were curious why the North Korean officer practically guided us to the South by taking us on their truck to the border. Here is the story. When my mother was interrogated about her attempt to escape, she said her husband was in the South and she was unable to support four children without a job. Asked about the four children, she said they were all girls. Immediately, the officer said, "then you better go to the South". Mother theorized that we five females—a mother and four girls—were less useful citizens for North Korea. We could only waste their precious short supply of rice and food. Is it an ironic fate or what?

At last, we arrived at the other side of the 38th parallel border. How relieved and happy we were! Soon a few young men at the border welcomed and led us to the nearby temporary house where other refugees were staying. The official refuge welcome center was 2 hours away to the south by car. It was already evening, and we had to stay at the temporary house over the night. We could have slept outside on the huge mat provided. To sleep inside, you had to pay. My mother decided to sleep outside to save money I supposed. During the night, however, it rained, and we had no choice but to move inside. So, my mother had to pay after all.

Having crossed the border into South Korea, our next goal was to find the refugee center in Chungdan City. This center was intended for all refugees from the North. While it would take two hours by car to reach the refugee center, on foot, it would take several hours to all day long. There was a charge for a truck ride. My mother told us to walk to save money since she had no idea when and how we could find my father. The only information my mother had was about one of my father's friends with his address, vaguely it was Shinsul-dong, a large section of the city of Seoul. Although I understood my mother's concern about the lack of money, I could not imagine I would walk again for hours with the baby on my back. I adamantly refused to walk any more. In fact, I could tell even my mother was also exhausted. So, we relented. Then, happily we decided to get on the truck. On the way by truck, we saw many of the refugees walking uphill road carrying the bags by hand or on their head. They looked all exhausted. It all took place on one day in late August 1948 (I do not remember the exact date).

At Chungdan refugee center, there were many newly pitched white tents spread over the wide ground. We were assigned to an empty tent. While we were so happy to have such space, now my mother began to worry about how to find my father. We had no idea how we were going to find him. The only connection we had was the person in Seoul about whom she heard from her relative.

My father, who was teaching in Inchon Middle School then, heard from one of his relatives that we were on the way to the South. Apparently, he came to the refugee center a couple of times to look for us and returned home disappointed. The day we arrived at the refugee center he missed the earlier train coming over. He was concerned that he might have missed us by the train that might have left earlier. He decided to take the next train and arrived 2 hours after we settled in the tent.

After putting things in the tent, my mother went to the nearby stream to wash some clothes and diapers. While we were playing outside of the tent excitedly, a gentleman was walking toward us with a slightly tilted hat, which was in fact a trait of my father. We immediately recognized him, and all of us ran toward him. It was a miracle! It was a miracle at that moment! Reuniting all our family in the refugee camp right after we arrived. I could not help but to believe it was God's grace. All night we could hear our parents talking quietly but joyously.

The next day, someone came to our camp. It was Mr. Choi, the director of the refugee camp. Mr. Choi was the father of a student whom my father taught in Shenyang years ago. My family was invited to dinner in his home. Mr. Choi and my father enjoyed reminiscing about their lives in Manchuria. After dinner, Mr. Choi took us to a large room and told us to take whatever we found necessary. There were tens of open cardboard boxes containing used but clean clothes and shoes. The letters CARE was marked on the box. These boxes were gifts from American people for refugees like us. There were jackets, dresses, and shoes. They were indeed precious gifts from the Americans at the time.

After miraculously reuniting with my father, we settled in Inchon City. My father taught at Inchon Middle School. My 7-year-old sister and I restarted elementary school. And, by the end of February 1950, I completed the first year in Sook-Myung Girls' Middle School in Seoul. For the entire year, I commuted from Inchon to Seoul by train. In March 1950, I started the second year of Middle school.

The Korean War broke out and Insurrection in Inchon

When the Korean War started on June 25, 1950, it was Sunday. While the radio announcer stated the news of the North Korean Army's invasion through the 38th parallel, it did not sound urgent. In the past, we used to hear about North Korea's aborted invasions off and on, or armed incursions of the border. My mother and I went shopping, and Mother bought me a new pair of sneakers. Next day, I went to school by train with new sneakers on. As soon we sat down in the classroom our homeroom teacher, bearing a grim expression, told us to go home and wait until further notice. We had no idea what that was all about.

At Seoul railroad station, I met my friend, Youngja. She was commuting from Inchon by train to attend Ewha Girl's Middle School which I already attended. We became good friends throughout the last year of school while commuting by the same train every day to school. We enjoyed giggling together so much when there was no school and plenty of time to play together. We made a pack to see each other when there was no school. We enjoyed it so much as though there was no trouble at all until then in our life. We were young innocent girls.

The following week, the radio announced that Seoul was taken by the advancing North Koreans troops, and the enemy was advancing southward to Inchon city. After the fall of Seoul, the capital, our South Korean Army was able to deter the further advance of the North Korean Army for over a week beyond the city of Seoul. The communists in Inchon City became impatient and started to be riotously violent. After taking over the Inchon City Hall, the rioters hoisted the North Korean Red Flag on the flagpole at the City Hall. Soon, we heard low flying airplanes. They were allied airplanes.

That day, I was visiting Youngja after a few days' no school. As usual, I had my younger sister, then 5 years old, with me. As the oldest daughter born with four younger sisters, it was my duty to look after at least one sister whenever I went out to play. While staying in Youngja's house, we heard the loud sound of airplane flying low and rapid machine gunshots nearby. I had to run back home. With my 6 years old sister on my back, I stepped outside and began to run. Suddenly one of the airplanes darted down with successive gunshots along the unpaved road, raising clouds of dust. I was only two feet away from the dust clouds. I heard someone shouting "get to the wall… lean on tightly against the wall! You could get killed." I ran toward the wall of a house along the road, sweating and panting. My sister on my back clung to me tight. At last, I was able to reach home. My mother, my father, my sisters, and the neighbors all came out from the underground shelter in the house, shouting with sighs of relief. My mother was in tears.

Late afternoon on that day, we heard the radio that the riot in the city was put down and the rioters were executed. Our neighbors including a girl of my age were going there to watch and, against my mother's objections, I joined the group also. Outside the wall of the city hall, a dozen straw sacks were scattered along the wall. Under each straw sack, two legs were exposed. People told us that they were the communist rioters.

A few more days passed when we heard on the radio that the enemy was approaching Incheon City. Not knowing what to pack, my mother first packed the rice bags and the food. My father carried the sewing machine on his back. Mother had the youngest, now 3 years old, and I oversaw my 6-year-old sister. All of us were carrying bags of all kinds for such emergencies. The neighbor, whom we used to call uncle, was a member of the anti-communist party. He and his colleagues used to punish the captured communists rather harshly and used to tell us his story. He looked in a panic, sweating heavily while carrying a big backpack. While we were walking along the road, there was a loud cannon shot and he fell and tumbled down the hill. His face was all wet and pale, frightened.

One day during our walk further south, we encountered armed North Korean soldiers for the first time. We were walking with other families who joined us on the way. One soldier noticed a young man among us. He interrogated the young man why he did not join the North Korean Army when all the young men were fighting in their units. He ordered us to go up the hill nearby. All of us were walking with two soldiers in the front and two in the back. Approaching the bottom of the hill, one soldier in front looked at us and asked, "Why are you all coming (with us)?" In the next moment, we found ourselves running away as fast as we could. My father said few days later, "When we were going toward the hill, my heart was beating so loud, and I felt like I heard the metallic sound of my heart banging against my chest wall." We heard later that an entire family of a young man were executed under the pretext of disobeying army recruitment by the young man. Finally, we arrived at a small village in the province of the Choong-Chung Book Do. One of my father's students lived there, my father remembered. After walking for the last three days continuously we were all exhausted. We decided to stay there for a while. Two days later, we learned that the North Korean Army had already passed the village and were marching further down to the South.

Renting a room of moderate size in front of the owner's house, we settled in. Another teacher from the same school my father worked at arrived a little later and rented a nearby house. Several days passed. One morning, a North Korean soldier knocked the door. He saw my father and asked him several questions. When he heard that my father was a teacher, he ordered him to go back to school in Inchon and start school. The other teacher was also ordered to leave for Incheon to continue teaching students. In fact, the soldiers already had the information about these two teachers. Thus, my father and the other teacher had to go back to school in Inchon. After my father left for Inchon, we kept hearing the air raids and bombing of the cities in that direction. We heard nothing from my father thereafter for over a month

In the regions, which was occupied by the North Korean army, there started a program to educate the people about North Korea. While the men were ordered back to their jobs, the women were summoned to a local town hall. One day, a young local village woman came by. She gathered about 20 women in the neighborhood. After a short introduction of herself and her mission of educating us about our new country, she asked us to follow her. After an hour's walk, we arrived at a local town hall. I remembered her having seen earlier. She was a nice young woman who used to work as a maid at someone's home in the village. She was kind, friendly and humble, as I remember.

Now, she had an armband around her left arm, which showed the North Korean flag. She said our country is North Korea and she would teach us the North Korea's National Anthem. After distributing the sheet with lyrics of the anthem, she sang one phrase (there was no musical instrument) and we followed the tune after her. When it came to repeating the same music, her tune of the same lyric was changed. It happened each time because she could not carry a tune correctly. No one learned the music after all.

Every day, my younger sister, Hie-sung, and I went out to collect dried twigs and tree branches for fuel to prepare the meals for my family. As time went by, we had to go deeper into the woods to gather wood. Often, I had to climb up the tree by embracing the tree trunk with both arms and legs, gradually climbing upward to reach the lowest dry branches of the tree. After I reach dry branches, I would break them off and let them fall to the ground, Hie-sung would collect them on the ground, and we brought them home together. During this process, my bare legs and arms were scratched by sharp twigs and poison ivy. The itchiness of my legs became intolerable, and I kept scratching through the night. Soon, the back of my both legs were covered with itchy blisters that turned into many ugly scabs. My legs were swollen.

One month later, after my father was sent back to Inchon. We did not hear a word from my father. We heard that the airplanes of allied forces bombed the city constantly. At last, my mother said "I have not heard from your father. I know Inchon has been bombarded constantly. We need to find out whether he is alive or not". There was another family nearby who was one of our old neighbors in Inchon and one teenage girl of hers also wanted to go. She was three years older (17-years-old) than I was and my mother felt relieved that she and I would be together.

Next day, with the lunch my mother made and a small amount of money, we girls started the three-day journey on foot toward Inchon. On the first day in the evening, we stayed in a local private home with minimum payment. As we walked all day for three days, by the time we neared the house where my father was supposed to be staying, I was unable to drag my severely swollen legs like those of an elephant. The house was on a small hill. I sat down sweating but was not able to lift my legs. The friend of mine accompanied with me went up ahead and soon I heard my father's voice as he was running down, calling my name. He sounded so pleased to see me and was happily surprised. I was so relieved that my father was alive!

We had a joyous evening with a simple dinner prepared by my father. By then I felt I was running a fever and very sleepy. All night I suffered from high fever, chills, and wet with sweat but I was so tired I fell sleep. My father was apparently so concerned and tried to wake me up, as I must be mourning with pain, but I continued to sleep. Next morning, still asleep, I heard my father's concerned voice calling me to wake me up or checking me to see if I was alright. As I opened my eyes, I saw my father's concerned expression and felt wet liquid over the calf of my left leg. The big abscess of the left leg had ruptured open. I guess it was probably infected. I might have had septicemia during the night. But thankfully, I soon recovered well.

Inchon Landing

Three days later, on September 15, 1950, the Incheon landing started under the command of General McArthur. At that time, I was not aware of this event. Nevertheless, from my father's reaction, he must have known and expected this invasion from the news. From the early morning, there was incessant loud bombing from the Inchon harbor. The family of a neighbor, my father and I sat squeezed inside the narrow underground shelter all day, listening to the squeaking cannon sounds from the gun boats of the Allied Navy in the Inchon Harbor. We were able to go out of the shelter for some relief. One time we heard a heavy metal piece dropping directly on the straw sack that covered the wooden panel that protected our underground shelter. The sack was right above where my father was sitting. A few hours later, the bombing sounds stopped for over an hour. My father went out. He found metal pieces that were still hot to touch. Soon we heard my father shouting, "All of you! Please, come out!"

Outside it was early in the evening. However, the sky was crimson red. We opened the window of the house, which was left empty all day, and looked down below. Since our house was on the hill, the city came into our sights and the entire city appeared to be on fire, with the flames dancing all over the place. The scene reminded me of the City of Rome in flame set by Nero in the movie "Quo Vadis".

Next day, South Korean soldiers were knocking every door and asked the people to come out. When the door of my house was knocked, we went out welcoming them. However, the soldiers looked tense by their facial expression and shouted, "Hands up!". They went into the house and searched every corner of the house. But the next day people were out in the marketplace for the first time. Everyone was busy going around and some were eating food sitting next to the cooking pot. I was also walking around in the market with a girl of the neighbor. Not far from the cooking and eating area, a charred man's body was lying on the ground. A part of his body was still smoking. Yet, people did not seem to be bothered by it, more preoccupied looking for things to buy. Someone must have the huge storage house break open and huge amounts of grains of rice were pouring out through the opened door into the street. People were busy gathering the rice with their hands in the bags.

Later, my mother returned to Inchon with my three sisters, and we were all reunited again.

Following the successful Incheon Landing, the enemies were rapidly chased back to the North. Every day was triumphant news of our side - South Korean, UN forces along with American - advancing to the north and at last almost to the northern border of North Korea, along Yalu River. However, before school started in September that year and we were about to settle down, we learned news that Mao Tsedong's Chinese army had joined the North Korean Army and crossed Yalu River and was moving down ruthlessly. With the planned strategic retreat by the UN forces, we also had to move to the further south, all over again.

To The South after Mao's Invasion

Since there was an arrangement of moving many people by the LST of the U.S. Navy, we were instructed to get ready and gathered at the Inchon Harbor where the LSTs were waiting. In the chilly January month of 1951, we were in line to embark on the LST after waiting for hours. With people packed inside the huge ship, it began to move and roll up and down. Many began to suffer from seasickness. By the time the ship reached the first harbor, Mokpo in Chul-na Nam Do, the LST stopped for a while. My mother said we should disembark the ship before we all die of seasickness. I was glad to get off the ship, too. Indeed, most passengers appeared exhausted from seasickness and left the ship.

After disembarking the LST, we were led to a school ground in the city. It was an elementary school. We were assigned to the classrooms. Each classroom was occupied by ten or more families. We slept on blankets brought from home. The next day, some ate food they brought, and others prepared their meals on the school ground using the small portable range they brought. Gradually, each family left the classrooms and settled in privately rented homes owned by locals one by one. We rented two rooms of a big house, and my father was hired as a teacher at the nearby girl's middle school. In the same house, across the hallway, a family of five lived. One girl of my age, 14 years old, of that family attended the same school as mine. However, as we heard her mother's constant coughing from the next room to ours, my mother became worried that the neighbor might have the consumption (TB). After several months living anxiously in the same house, we decided to move out to another rented home. Luckily, we did not catch that dreadful germ.

During our stay in Mokpo, the war stopped as an armistice in 1953. We returned to Incheon City where my father taught in the Inchon Boys' Middle School and became the vice principal of the school. We returned to our respective elementary and middle schools in Inchon until 1954 when our family moved to Seoul after my father became a teacher of Ewha Gils' High School.

The Korean War That I witnessed as a teenage

Richrd Suhung Hann, M.D.

Prologue

When the Korean War started, I was 14 years of age and was in my second year in middle school. I was born in the city of Hamhung, and World War II ended five years earlier, in 1945. The Soviet Red Army was the first foreign military force to reach the city of Hamhung with regular soldiers and all its high-ranking brasses. Hamhung used to be the stronghold of the Canadian Presbyterian Missionaries which built the Jehye Hospital, Yeongsaeng Boys and Girls High Schools before the Japanese Imperial Power drove them out in 1942. The Canadian Presbyterian Mission impacted greatly for the Protestantism in Korea with the supporting Korean Nationalism, and for the education for young Korean physicians, preachers, businessmen and so forth.

The Soviet troops entered the city of Hamhung on August 24, 1945, with no resistance. Two days later, Kim Il-sung was instated in Pyongyang by the Soviets. Apparently, he was hand-picked by Josef Stalin, the General Secretary of the Communist Party of Soviet Union. The implanting soviet system in North Korea was completed by September 1948, by the cunning and ruthless efforts of Terenti Shtykov then Soviet ambassador to North Korea, who acted more like the supreme ruler of North Korea.

By early months of 1949, the North Korean leader Kim Il-sung realized that the communist guerrillas he had dispatched to

South Korea were facing a strong resistance by the South Korean forces, and the North Korean guerrillas needed a full-scale resuscitation by the North Korean forces. According to the Soviet Union's official newspaper Krasnaya Zvezda (Red Star), Kim Il-sung went to Moscow to meet Joseph Stalin and entreated the permission to invade South Korea. Initially Stalin strongly objected. He said he would approve if the South Korea attacked the North Korea by force. Kim then turned to China. On May 14, 1949, he informed the Soviet ambassador to North Korea, T.F. Shtykov that Mao had agreed to an immediate return of two of the three ethnic Korean divisions to North Korea. From these early days, Kim was playing the China card to move Kremlin. It turned out that Mao Zedong said, "not in the near future such advance is advisable since Chinese Communists were still tied down with the Nationalists forces." Kim was again pressing Stalin in September of 1949 and in January of 1950, when the Chinese Liberation reached its conclusion of the initial goal. Kim was very crafty in his actions at these instances, considering the psychology of the Soviet leader, who was apprehensive of the growing influence and independence of Mao, who is to become the master of the great Chinese continent including Manchuria. Without having intelligence of all these, the United States began to withdraw its troops from South Korea in June of 1949. It became more certain to Stalin's mind that the belligerent President Rhee of South Korea would strike the North Korea first. Moreover, Dean Acheson, U.S. Secretary of State, dropped the Korean Peninsula and Formosa from the all-important "defense perimeter" of the U.S. on his speech of January 22, 1950, before the National Press Club. Stalin thought that the U.S. would not interfere with the North Korean advance and that Kim would be able to overrun the South completely. In April 1950, Stalin told Kim that 'due to the changing international situation' he would agree to Koreans moving towards unification, 'but if China did not agree, the decision must be postponed.' Kim visited Moscow again in May 1950, when he voiced his confidence that the U.S. would not interfere in such a conflict and if the Japanese send in their forces, then China would come to the aid of North Korea.

By early 1950s, North Korea amassed massive invasion forces of a total of 379 tanks, 264 Yat fighters, 188 bombers, 200 artillery tubes from the Soviet Union. Mao sent two divisions of ethnic Korean soldiers to Kim, most of which stayed outside of military camps due to the shortage of facility.

Suddenly, many military officers became visible in our neighborhood. My friend's house boarded several of Korean Chinese officers who were trying to learn colloquial language. They were quite friendly and tried to be very polite. At night, tanks were rolling in groups along the highway from the Hamhung Division Headquarter to the railroad station. It is a great pity that western intelligence had missed all these movements in the early months of 1950. Obviously, Joseph Stalin changed his mind, considering the changing pattern of international situations and his own confidence on his domestic strength by ending American monopoly on nuclear arsenal in addition to his ambition of exporting his communist ideology outside of Eurasian continent by using the young brash Kim as a test case of his grand old scheme.

On June 20, 1950, Shtykov informed Moscow that at least 20:00 hours Moscow time, the North had intercepted orders saying that the South would commence hostility against the North at 2300 hours. The next day, Kim informed Stalin via the Soviet embassy that the South had been given the news about a prospective offensive by the Korean People's Army. In this communiqué, he also noted that he would begin combat operation precisely on the 25th. To cover up the plan of imminent invasion, Kim floated false narratives such as the North was about to release a staunch anti-communist Christian leader Jo Man-shik to the South, but the South Korean Army attacked the Northern territory at three different locations.

Invasion

On June 25, 1950 (local time), North Korea launched a massive attack across the entire length of 38th Parallel with invasion forces of more than 90,000 North Korean and Chinese troops, along with over 50 Soviet-supplied T-34 tanks smashing hard the under-armed and unprepared South Korean border troops.

The U.S. Central Intelligence had concluded an invasion was unlikely days earlier. As you know, the US observers had inspected the border two days earlier when the South Korean President Syngman Rhee warned them that the invasion was imminent. The South Korean and U.S. forces were totally unprepared. The South Korean troops did not have any tank, anti-tank weapon or artillery that could halt the North Korean forces. Within two days, the South Korean troops had abandoned the defense north of Seoul, the capital of Republic of Korea. On the third day of the war, Kim's tanks rolled into Seoul without any organized resistance.

Within three days of starting the War, Kim's Army sacked and entered the city of Seoul. But the timing was wrong. The Soviet ambassador to the U.N. had been boycotting over the matter of Communist China's representation in the Security Council. Soon, U.S. President Truman was informed of the invasion from Secretary of State Dean Acheson. President Trauma instantly resolved to repel the aggression. On June 25,

1950, the United Nation Security Council (UNSC) unanimously condemned the North Korean invasion of South Korea by the UNSC resolution 82. Two days later, Resolution 83 was announced recommending member states to send military assistance to South Korea. Why the representative of the USSR was not in the counsel? It was puzzling. At the same time, President Truman ordered General MacArthur to transfer military materials to the South Korean Army while providing air cover to evacuate U.S. nationals. Within a few weeks of the invasion, B-29 bombers appeared in the skies of Hamheung and dropped bombs targeting the longest bridge over the Sungcheon River, not too far from my home. The citizens of Hamheung were so afraid that most of them hit the road to move to countryside to take refuse from the bombardments.

I was assigned to take my two nephews and two nieces to their maternal grandparents who lived across the river by the bridge. The raiders missed the target and killed several people down on the sandy beach. We walked along the bank of the Sungcheon River northwards for two hours to reach the destination, the home of my aunt. Once unloaded those kids, I headed alone for my aunt's orchard, which was my most favorite resort where I spent most of my summer vacation. Fruits were plenty around. In the next door, I had a good friend of mine, Park Jungdae. We used to enjoy practicing Neopolitan songs.

In early August, a group of B-29 appeared from the Southern sky and raided Hungnam Chemical Plant for several hours. Black smoke had been rising into the sky for several days. That industrial complex was the largest of its kind in Northeast Asia. Then, a few weeks later, a squadron of B-29 came in three waves and raided Hamheung Army Headquarter and barracks. Black smoke rose above the mountains ridge which covered the northern site. The house of my parents was very close to the target. I was so afraid. I rushed to go home. I waded across the Sungcheon River, climbed up the mountains and ran to the house. Everybody was safe, but the house was damaged, losing portions of ceilings.

Incheon Landing

By mid-August, Kim's forces pushed the U.N. allied forces and Republic of Korean troops into the southeastern corner of the Peninsula, which was protected by the Nak-dong River. In fact, it was called "Busan Perimeter". It means a small city size of the peninsula was in the hands of allies. But miraculously by the reinforcement of the U.S. 8th Army and regrouped Republic of Korea divisions of army, advance of the North Korean forces was halted there. At the same time, General MacArthur launched an amphibious landing at Inchon and recaptured Seoul on September 19 swiftly and sacked Kim's troops, which rapidly disintegrated and began to retreat to the North.

On October 1, the UN Command authorized operations north of the 38th parallel. The ROK (Republic of Korea)'s 1st Corps advanced north through the Eastern Front and the Central Front. On October 7, the U.S. Eighth Army and ROK Army 1st Division pushed up the Western Front and captured Pyongyang, the capital of North Korea, on October19, 1950. In the Eastern Front, ROK 1st Corps captured Wonsan on October 10, and Hamheung on October 17. The U.S. Marine 1st Division landed on Wonsan on October 25, and advanced to the northern highland.

My brother Soo-in just turned 18 and was to graduate from the Hamheung Normal School in two weeks. With the graduation, he knew that the Communist Party would conscript him on the spot. He went into hiding with his classmate at his country home about 20 miles west of Hamheung. We sent him some books for him. For over three months, he was able to hide, and my father was able to visit him a couple of times. Soon, he heard that the U.N. forces were coming up to the area and likely liberating the area. Soon after he heard the news, he came out from hiding to enjoy the fresh air. No sooner than he came out, a group of retreating North Korean soldiers spotted him, arrested, and dragged him to the Hamheung Security Headquarter. There were several dozens of draft-dodgers already waiting for sundown. As soon as dusk came down, these draft-dodgers were led by several security officers to the north. Soo-in, the brother of mine, slowed his pace and took the last row. He found the moment he could avoid the watchful eyes of the soldier and the group was turning at a corner of the street he ran away through the familiar hometown alleys. He was able to reach home safely. The whole family was so relieved. My father came to the orchard the next day to take me home. Up to that evening, our family was all lucky.

Two days later, my older brother Soo-heong brought home one of our remote cousins who went to the South a few years earlier and returned with the advancing ROK troops. With him a soldier, a full Sergeant of the ROK army, stayed with us overnight. Two of them talked all night about their lives in the South. It was full of hardship, which rendered an instant de-ja-vu as if it was my own doing. What an eerie thing it was! Next day I went downtown to the school with Soo-in and saw a sign said, "English Class." We registered without hesitation, and I attended every day for about four weeks, hoping I could converse with the American soldiers. I practiced my primitive English whenever possible.

President Rhee's visit in Hamheung

In the middle October of that year, President Syngman Rhee visited Hamheung and made a big speech in front of the large crowd, hundreds. He was with entourages of several dozens of dignitaries, both Korean and American, including Captain Alexander Haig, several U.S. military's brasses and Dr. Hyun Bong-Hak, who worked as General Almond's liaison for civil affairs. I do remember some of the President's speeches. "Everybody, people from the south, people from the north, and the people from the east and west must work together to make our country strong and prosperous. Let us build a great country enviable globally… In case our allies must evacuate, I will make sure that even your dog can be accompanied with you".

However, I could not imagine the mighty U.S. forces would retreat, but I even wondered why he would say such a thing. Nonetheless, the Communist China issued its own intention to enter the Korean War several times through various diplomatic channels. Mao Zedong, who watched the U.S. 1st Marine Division landing on Wonsan, trembled with fear that they even might enter the China one day also. On October 8, Mao appointed Peng Duhuai the commander of the Chinese forces in Korea and renamed the forces as the "Chinese Peoples Voluntary Army" (PVA) and ordered 200,000 PVA men to enter North Korea in secret on October 25. The Chinese PVA marched "dark-to-dusk" to avoid exposure to the U.S. aerial reconnaissance.

October 1950, the US Command completely misjudged the situation to such an extent that the General MacArthur's Command issued a "Offense for Home by Christmas" to all fronts. On November 24, 1950, the US Eighth Army launched an advance along the Northwest corridor, while the US X corps were advancing along the Northeastern corridor, and the US 1st Marine Division was pushing the North Korean troops to the Chinese border. A friend of mine, Baek Kee-soo was a second lieutenant of the ROK Army when the Korean War broke out.

His division spearheaded to the north up to the Aprok (Yalu) River. He led his platoon into the hamlet where he grew up and met several kins. He told me later. When he went to the bank of the Aprok (Yalu) River he found his platoon was surrounded by the Chinese PVA and became prisoners of war. Three years later he was released from the camp during the prisoners-swap. Much later he came to live in U.S.

Starting with a surprise attack on October 25, 1950, on the ROK 1st Division on the Western Front, the Chinese PVA 39th Army encircled and attacked the US 9th Cavalry Regiment around Unsan on November 1. Several Corps of the Chinese PVA were deployed near the Jangjin Lake (Chosin Lake) by November 27th. The Battle of the Chosin Lake began, and on December 13th, about 30,000 US troops broke through the Chinese siege in the Kaema Highland and successfully withdrew to Hamheung, decimating two Chinese PVA's elite Corps along the redeployment.

General MacArthur ordered the withdrawal from Hungnam. On December 13, all troops of the US 10th Corps gathered to Hungnam with the US 1st Marine at the head and evacuation from Hungnam. The 121 Evacuation Hospital moved from Hamheung to the Ainsworth Naval Hospital Ship, where the nursing staff of the 1st Mobile Army Surgical Hospital (MASH) also joined.

Refugees Outnumbered the Troops

ROK First Corps commanding officer Major General Kim Baek-il planned to provide safe-passages of the refugees through Wonsan port via the east corridor. However, the Chinese People's Volunteer Army (PVA) quickly sacked the port city.

Refugees appeared first when the US 1st Marine started to redeploy to the South. Suddenly, hundreds of refugees, most of the Hamheung citizens, gathered. The US troops blocked the main route from Hamheung to Hungnam for fear of enemy infiltration. On December 15, General Kim Baek-il discussed the refugee-evacuation matter with the US Tenth Corps commander, General Almond, who suggested that 4 to 5 thousand civilians could be transported by train from Hamheung to Hungnam harbor. The ROK Marine provided two Tank Landing Ships (LST). Not knowing about the transport, my older brother Soo-heung decided to walk to Hungnam. Only three brothers left home and arrived at the Yong-dae bridge, but the route was completely closed to refugees. Not knowing the situation, we waited there all day and came home after sundown to the surprise of my family. My father must have sensed what was waiting for the family. My father was not talking at all.

In dawn, next day, three of us, brothers, left home, again not realizing that it was the last time to see the family. We went upstream of the Horeon River and crossed the Jeongneung bridge, and then we walked down the trail leading to the Hungnam waterfront. A UN soldier at a checkpoint stopped us and asked various questions about us. It was a black soldier, and I answered to him with my newly attained primitive English. He gave us an easy pass. After walking a couple of hours, we came to the crowded waterfront where tens of thousands of refugees were waiting. About 200 warships were moored in the Hamheung Sound of the East Sea. There was only occasional gunfire from the ship. After waiting a few hours in the local school ground, we walked to the home of my cousin and stayed there overnight. My cousin was an engineer at Hungnam Chemical Factory which was destroyed by the raid.

Much later, we heard that people remaining in the school ground were suspected of as enemy infiltrators and dumped to the other side of the Sungcheon River and even opened fire on them.

The next day, we went to the waterfront very early in the morning. Then a few hours later, a huge LST arrived at the pier and opened its wide jaw. People started to board in a queue and loading ended later in the afternoon. We got a small space in the hull. Immediately I went up to the deck and looked around. The deck was also filled up with standing room only. The darkness fell rather quickly. Some naval vessels in the bay began to fire their long guns. Finally, the battleship Missouri began to fire loudly. The trajectory was glaringly in the direction of my home! However, I knew that I was not able to stop it but just to pray. My heart ached. Self-defense was no longer honored here. Many years later, I heard from someone who came from the town where we were, the house my father stayed in was hit. The actual targets must have been the military headquarters and barracks. My family went down to the basement, and nobody was hurt. The more I thought about it the more I was so uncomfortable as though I could have done something to protect my family. I felt sorry for what I had done to my father and my mother, and I could not do for the rest of my family. Remorse was inevitable but regret was not correctable.

Decades later, it became very obscure who had decided to take care of the refugees. I thought President Syngman Rhee in consultation with General MacArthur made the decision to bring refugees to Geoje Island and he had arranged the policing provision days before the LSTs were there. However, a few actors started to claim the honor for themselves after those big shots all passed aways. I always thought that in an ideological war like this, they should think of the refugee matters seriously. Large chunks of the population have shifted from the North to the South in search of freedom. The same phenomenon happened in the South when they were occupied for only 3 months by the North Korean troops. We do recall that Leonard LaRue, the captain of the now famous cargo ship S.S. Meredith Victory, making the decision to evacuate as many as 14,000 refuge on his ship. It was a cargo ship that supplied fuel for the war effort. How one cargo ship could have so many people. Some say the size of the ship and the number of the refugees do not match. He navigated through the winter water of the Pacific Ocean to supply aviation fuel to a marine airfield near Hungnam. When he arrived there, the airfield had been closed. All he saw was the people left behind on the piers. In addition to some volatile cargo loaded already he took as many people as possible in his ship and carried them to safety. The ship was later renamed as the "Ship of Miracles." Captain LaRue entered a monastery to became "a monk of St. Paul" I heard that he might become a candidate to be canonized. I wish he would be canonized.

Thus I Crossed the 38th Parallel

The LST, the landing ship of the US Navy I was on, was loaded with over 9,000 people, five times the capacity and slowly steering out of the congested bay, where over 200 ships were mooring in the evening of December 22. The black curtain of the wintery darkness descended rather quickly over the horizon. Long guns started to fire from the several ships, lighting the vast bay. Judging from its trajectory, the PLA was moving quickly to choke down the siege of the retreating allied forces. Later I learned that when the PLA entered the city of Hungnam on December 25, 1950, the city was completely empty.

As the LST moved further away from the bay, the waves became rougher, and the big ship began rocking back and forth and side to side. I started to feel sick to my stomach and tried to calm down to fight the motion sickness by facing the cold air of the north. Many people were feeling the urge and I threw up everything I ate for lunch. There was no water to drink and no place to sit. Looking up at the dark sky and black sea alternately for several hours I heard a sailor shouting that "we are crossing the 38th parallel". It was around 6 AM on 23rd of December. Cheers of relief were heard everywhere. I went down from the deck and joined my brothers, and we were kind of relieved momentarily but quickly entangled with guilty feeling.

Slowly I started to worry how to survive in the strange land. I thought my older brother Soo-heung could take care of us all, but things can turn out quite odd way. Moments later, I was thinking of ideological aspects of the two competing societies. But my limited experience did not allow me to advance any further. I decided to read more to justify my move.

I believed the war would end within three to six months. Thus, we will go back home and the whole family will be reunited as before. What a simplistic thinking it was. I often laugh at myself wondering how naïve I was. However, I did not want to discuss this with anybody.

The ship was navigating slowly but steadily along the east coast lines and around Busan, and further South to the destination. It was about 4 or 5 pm on December 24 when we arrived at Jangseungpo, the southern port of Geoje Island. The weather was much milder than in the north.

A long procession of refugees filled the main street along the waterfront and was being led to a local public school. Suddenly, someone greeted us by calling "Hyongnim". It was Mr. Lee Bong-joo who was recently transferred as Surveillance Chief of the Geoje Police Station by the order of President Syngman Rhee. He was born in Jangjin highland and occasionally came down to Hamheung and met my elder brother several times. He was a very strong anti-communist and he moved to the South many years back and joined the Police Forces to fight the communist underground dispatched by Kim Il-sung along and came to continue his specialty here in Geoje Island.

Thousands of refugees were detained in the school yard and spent their first night in the South on the school grounds. Fortunately, it was much warmer than the North. I woke up early in the morning at the unusually loud church bell of the Christmas Day. Not knowing the importance of Christmas, I was concerned with the long journey we might have to make that day. After consulting some friends, we decided to stay in Janseungpo. A few days later, Mr. Lee Bong-joo arranged our stay at his residence. Soo-in got a job as a security guard at a local UN Aid Agency. Within a few weeks in the job, he felt ill with epidemic typhus. With a few doses of antibiotics, he recovered from it and he decided to enter the National Guard Military Academy.

In the meanwhile, Mr. Lee Bong-joo moved to a better house and my big brother and I joined Mr. Lee in his new residence. Then, I started to attend the Geoje Middle School which was run by the Presbyterian Foundation. This was the first time I was exposed to the Christianity. It was not that easy task for an atheist to accept Christianity. I struggled a lot at first.

On December 26, 1950, General Matthew Ridgway assumed the Command of the US Eight Army following the death of General Walton Walker in a traffic accident.

In the meanwhile, Seoul fell into the control of the PVA and, on January 16, 1951, the North Korean Army Command was merged into the PVA. Kim Il-sung resisted it but was pushed out. Now, Kim, being relieved from the commanding job, started to personally orchestrate trumped-up charges against his potential rivals, and eventually purged them one by one.

In April 1951, General MacArthur was relieved from the U.S. Supreme Commander, which was then assumed by General Ridgway, who pushed the PVA to the north of 38th parallel by May 20, 1951. And then the stalemate started, which lasted until the armistice of the Korean War in 1953.

General Ridgway was also authorized to use nuclear arsenals if a major direct attack originates from outside of Korean territory. In October 1951, US Air Force B-29 bombers practiced bombing runs from Okinawa to North Korea. An envoy was sent to Hong Kong to deliver a warning to China, Next month Stalin and Zhou En-lai agreed the exchange of POWs and peace negotiations started.

In retrospect, the U.S. should have used the nukes to terminate Kim's regime which was illegal from the outset and was not approved by the United Nation. The regime was created by Stalin.

On June 18, 1953, six weeks before the Armistice Agreement was signed, the much-disappointed President Rhee set free 27,389 anticommunist KPA prisoners of war and pressed the U.S. to forge the Mutual Defense Treaty between South Korea and the United States, which was later achieved.

My sister's brother-in-law Lee Nak-byn was studying medicine at Hamheung Medical College when he was conscripted to the Korean People's Army at the outset of the War. He became prisoner of war and freed by President Rhee. He resumed his medical education at the Jeon-nam Medical College and became an internist in the South.

However, millions of North Korean refugees waited and waited for the day of reunification, which has never arrived. Many of them moved out of the Geoge Island and dispersed into the countryside. The influx of labor forces indeed helped bring the "Miracle of Han River" initiated by President Rhee and completed by Park Chung-hee. The Republic of Korea became a world-level economic power in a short period of time from the ashes of the Korean War. Both Samsung and Hyundai have built huge shipyards in Geoje Island and many automobile factories were erupted all over the South. The South Korea became one of the largest Christian Democratic country in Asia.

Epilogue

The recent Russian invasion to Ukraine has shown that even a leading nuclear power could not occupy a small, militarily inferior neighboring democratic country at will. The Ukrainian people have shown an exceptional courage and unity to fight back and hold on the ground. The mistaken invasion has united European states even closer militarily and economically. It is an awesome display of free world to fight off the autocracy and command economy which represent Russia, China and North Korea no matter how much WMDs they possess.

As the Ukrainian war protracts further and longer, the Russians will suffer from economic downturn and eventually find out that their loss would be as great or greater than that of Ukraine.

A new world order is about to emerge from this war. The Communist China has reaffirmed their support for Russia. They are on the wrong side of history. North Korea began to see that their nukes are of little value no matter how much they improve their nuclear arsenal.

As a result of this war, the NATO is about to expand to Finland and Sweden, and the European Union is to have Ukraine as its member. Free World is getting ready to adopt two-China policy, and step-up the sanctions against the rogue regimes such as North Korea and Iran.

The US President Joseph Biden agreed with the newly elected South Korean President Yoon Suk-yeol that the two allies to resume their joint military exercise in response to the threat from the North, and the "US will respond decisively to any threat and any aggression" said State Department spokesman Ned Price.

According to the South Korean Science Ministry, South Korea successfully launched a surveillance satellite to the orbit of 435 miles on June 21, through a three-stage Nuri rocket from Goheung "Nara Space Center" on its southwestern island. The launch made South Korea the world's 10th nation to place a satellite into the space with its own technology.

This marks that South Korea can monitor the North's nukes which are of little value no matter how much they innovate the arsenals. South Korea plans to put on four more Nuri satellites in coming years. The successful launch is very meaningful since the rocket can be converted into long-range missiles when a warhead is mounted with a reentry capability. As long as the hostile powers like China and Russia are there, South Korea has to develop long-range missiles as well.

North Korea is expected to detonate another nuclear device sooner or later, according to some experts. Should they experiment another nuclear device, then South Korea and Japan should be allowed to possess their own nuclear arsenal. That is the most effective way of stopping North Korea from venturing any further.

Ukrainians have shown many important lessons to the world; the importance of the national mobilization, and the fighting spirit and courage to defend their own land using geographical knowledge. In addition, the Republic of Korea needs more comprehensive surveillance, covert and overt, over the North Korean territory, and massive preemptive strikes as well as a counter-attack capability.

The Republic of Korea doesn't deserve another military conflict with the North Korea but the two should be reunited peacefully as a free democracy with rolling market economy. The North Koreans are not serfs for Kim family. They should be unshackled from the reign of terror as soon as possible. Time is running out. On July 6, 2022, President Yoon ordered the Military of South Korea to punish North Korea swiftly and firmly in the event it carries out a provocation. The operational plans clearly stipulate "Massive Punishment and Retaliation to incapacitate the North Korean leadership in a major conflict by mobilizing the Kill Chain Preemptive Strike".

The 6.25 Korean War and I

Kyung-Joo Lee/ Poet

6.25 War broke out when I was in college. I immediately enlisted in the 7th Division of the Army of Republic of Korea in Uijeong-bu as a student soldier after the North Korean tanks entered the capital city of Seoul, within three days of the war. My unit of the 7th Division of the Army retreated through Chang-dong, Miari, and Goopabal of the outskirt of the Seoul, the capital city of Korea. We retreated all the way to the Nak-dong River.

South Korea, where only part of the cities of Daegu and Busan were left unoccupied by the north Korean military within a short period of North Korean invasion, was in danger of a complete capture by the North Korean Army. Fortunately, the U.N. forces were quickly organized and able to resist at the critical points along the Nakdong River, southeast corner of the peninsular. It was one of the fiercest fighting of the war and both sides suffered a huge number of casualties. The entire defense line, formed along the Nakdong River by the U.S. 8th Army under the command of General Walker was able to resist until the change of the feature of the war took place in September 1950. At the same time the moral of the allied forces and Korean forces increased rapidly. After the successful Inchon landing under the command of General Douglas MacArthur, allied forces moved fast chasing the North Korean forces until Allied forces reached the Yalu River. The morale of the Korean military and allied forces was high as expected. General MacArthur's victory in the Incheon landing operation was successful although there were some doubts lingering.

With the establishment of the 1st Corps of the Republic of Korean Army, I became a staff of the ROK 8th Infantry Division's headquarters. My unit moved to Dongdu-cheon, Uijeong-bu, Sari-won, and Pyeongyang, and then to Hui-cheon in North Pyongan Province. We were very near the Yalu River. Then, we heard that the 22nd Regiment of our division was fighting the Chinese army and struggling hard. The front became complex in new awakening. The Chinese military with massive humanity were mobilized and they were approaching the Yalu River quite quickly. At that time, I received a special enlistment from the Army General School on November 12, 1950, in Dongrae, Busan. The city of Busan was so crowded with refugees, recently landed allied soldiers, and refugee transient government of Republic of Korea. Indeed, the city of Busan was in a big mess.

Dong-lae was famous for its hot springs and the scenery, it was also an educational city with elementary, middle, and high schools clustered around it. But during the war, all those school buildings were occupied by the allied forces. On November 12, 1950, in the school building which became the 14th Army General School, 250 people took their oath of service. The students started the education for officers' candidacy. I was one of them. The training was harsh, and it was particularly a very cold winter. Army General Kim Hong-il was the school president. He is remembered as Vice-Chancellor. I was in the 18th in the class, and I made close relationship with Kim Gak-gyu, who was the 19th. It was an unusually cold winter. There was a lot of snow even in Busan, but the chilly winter rain was much more unbearable.

The very hard training was continued, whether it was raining or snowing. The cadets wearing an unfitting U.S. overcoat, unfitting large American army boots that did not fit the feet, carrying the heavy M1 rifle, but we were carrying a strong tight fellowship and friendship, and singing military marches encouraged us with pride on that harsh training ground. The training ground was near the top of the hill which had to face the cold wind from the ocean through Haeundae beach. We were fed rice and kimchi in a crumpled aluminum bowl. We had to wake up at five in the morning with a hungry stomach. The first meal we had to take was steamed barley meals with bean sprout soup.

Like the steel is melted in a blast furnace to be shaped for something useful, we were shaped to be army officers. In the shortest training period of less than 3 months, the beginner commander, the second lieutenant of the army, was smelted and received a badge of the rank. On January 14, 1951, I graduated from the Army General School with the 14th class. At the time, the launch of our comprehensive school was called metaphorically as 'school for the consumable or expendable first officers.'

On January 16 of that year, I received the order for the post of Special Forces (A) No. 54 at the Daegu Army Headquarters. They said it was like the end of this world. Kim Gak-gyu, one of my classmates was killed in a battle as a platoon commander of the 1st Division in his first venture. Another classmate of mine, Lieutenant Dongkwan Shin and 49 other members of the 7th Division received a special assignment and headed to the Yeongwol region where the 7th Division is stationed. At that time, Kim Gak-gyu was attached to the 3rd Corps of the 7th Division. He was carrying out a sweeping operation against the remnants of the People's Army in the Hongcheon-Chuncheon region. I was again assigned to the position as the commander of the 3rd Platoon, 1st Company, 3rd Battalion. With the guidance of the company's senior officer, I was introduced to the platoon member as 'a new platoon commander.' Most of my platoon members were new recruits with no combat experience either and with limited education, a rookie second lieutenant who had completed an ultra-short-term education with no experience in conducting leadership. And two liaison officers were my high school classmates who also volunteered to enlist. I then realized that all those comrades are naïve boys, novice soldiers but were army officers. We all had lively personalities like the baby boy of a family who were so naïve and playful but did not have any idea what the war like and they carried out their assignment like some sort of play with the playful spirit. During the break, the two liaison officers made jokes and entertained the soldiers of the platoon. They became our platoon jokesters. To the two men, just only two years older than I was, I had the special feeling, like I would have with my brothers. I carried the feeling for a long time.

At the end of January 1951, not long after I was appointed as a platoon commander, the People's Army of the North had built a strong defensive position at the Nokjeon-ri, about 18 km southeast of Yeongwol, right in front of the 7th Division. They were fighting with all their might to stop or delay the pursuit of the enemy. This mountain nearby was so steep and rough that it was very exhausting to climb when the snow was accumulating more than 80 cm and the temperature was dropping.

The 3rd Platoon and the 2nd Platoon progressed in tandem. The enemy, literally holding our life, surprised us once more with the sudden bombardment by the new attacks. It was again a surprise attack. The new recruits who had very little combat experience were surprised and did not know what to do, and they could not even raise their heads properly. In addition, as the enemy snipers pulled the trigger with the aimed shot, the damage loss was great, and the blood of the red covered the white snow all over the place.

This was my first battle that I commanded as a platoon commander. In fact, it was also my first battle for life or death. And yet I was not afraid at all. The flashed in my mind momentarily was that the lives of 30 soldiers under my command depended on me. If I did not kill the enemy, they would kill me. I had the thought flashed that I had to win this battle and secure a favorable situation for the advancement of the allies. Surprising was also the idea that we live or die in the battle that is the fates of soldiers. We were in the war.

While maintaining an attack formation with the 2nd platoon, suddenly the contact with the 2nd platoon commander was lost. I immediately reported the situation to the company commander by radio. Meanwhile I ordered the troops of the 2nd Platoon to be under my command. Meanwhile the enemy's stubborn deterrence resulted in many casualties of my troop. The advance became more and more difficult. With all my might, I tried to control the platoon as best as I could. There was the sound of a short, muffled cry "Private Park!" But the soldier was about ten yards below the small ridge. By the time I reached him he was covered with blood all over the chest and I could only see the white part of his eyes. I cried "Private Park! Private!" There was no answer. The private Park's last words were "I'm a platoon man!" I bit my teeth and said, "yes, I will avenge for you!" He shouted and stared at the enemy with bloodshot eyes before he closed his eyes. However, in that battle, sadly, the battle was unfavorable for us. Sadly, we were pushed back by the enemy's irresistible counterattack, and we retreated.

War is truly miserable. It is more so when one nation suffered millions of casualties due to bloody battles between the same people as a family feud. The people of North Korea and South Korea are one people, one history, one ethnicity. This country was destroyed, Korea was destroyed. The 7th Division recaptured Yeongwol again in late January 1951, by advancing to the north along the Jeongseon-Pyeongchang-axis line and securing the rugged mountains on both sides of the only route possible for maneuvering and leading to the east coast (Pyeongchang-Soksari-Gangneung).

On March 12, 1951, in this battle, I was severely injured on my stomach and both arms. I was transferred to the 36th Army Hospital in Busan. I was in the hospital for four months, until July, and then I was assigned to be the commander of the 83rd Army Unit (Wonho Battalion) Daegu Detachment Company. Army Unit 83 was a unit that was to accommodate the disabled soldiers, injured by the war such as blindness, loss of limbs and so forth severely that they need assistance in many aspects. They lived uncomfortable lives. They all received a special discharge from the military and in general they all go back to their hometown as the wounded soldiers.

On September 10, 1951, I was also discharged as an honored warrior. That was the end of my brief military career, and a consumable officer of the Allied Army. Even though my military career was short, I am assured by the fact that I devoted my youth to protect my country and achievement in creating the foundation for the advancement of my country. That is a great reward for me with the pride and the honor of serving my country. And that gives me the pride of my life until today and will be for the rest of my life. Even now, on the 72nd anniversary of the outbreak of 6.25 Korean war, the 69th anniversary of the armistice, the memory of the shout of "Platoon Commander" and the voice of Park Il-byeong (private) touch my heart. [1]

---

[1] *Six months ago, I approached poet Kyung-Ju Lee to document his firsthand experience of the 6.25 Korean War. He graciously agreed to my request. Unfortunately, he was diagnosed with laryngeal cancer, which prevented him from completing the task. In his message, he expressed his efforts to gather relevant materials and resume writing but was unable to fulfill his original plan. However, he entrusted me, as his editor, to utilize his previously written memoir of the 6.25 battle.*

Memories, My Random Thoughts, of 1950 Korean War

Seung-Kyoon Park, M.D.

My hesitation in writing this story comes with a realization that no matter how awful it may sound, my experiences during the war cannot be compared to those of many others of my generation. This relative 'nonstory' is coming to light only from the urgings of my friend, Dr. Chang-Wuk Kang, who persuaded me to believe that every piece of our experiences may be of value to the future generations in some ways.

Cholwon (Gangwon Province)

Fate is not decided by one's birthplace. But it may remain as lingering forces in one's life and exerts its influences in various ways, often unexpectedly. Cholwon where I was born is located about 10 miles north of the 38th Parallel (38,1466-degree N). The earliest years of my life were spent in that quiet and peaceful farming village not far from Cholwon. I lived with my maternal grandparents since my father had to go to work in Tianjin, China. Without my parents, I was a shy and severely introverted child. I owe my surviving childhood entirely to my grandma's single-minded care and devotion. Without any formal education, she nevertheless earned the villagers' admiration for her good heart and generosity. Probably due to a constant fear that I, a sole reminder of her bloodline, might also fall victim to the scourges of tuberculosis or other infectious diseases, she did everything to protect me from early death. Two of my male cousins did not survive beyond age three. I was a lonely child, but my grandma's love gave me comfort and assurance. It would be great if the whole world loved you. But if you have one person who truly loves you, it is just about enough for you to stand up and go on living. At age five I started going to Japanese kindergarten in Woljong Ri near Cholwon. But soon I moved to Seoul because my father had returned from China and found a job in Seoul. I first enrolled at Ansan Elementary School not far from Seodaemun(West Gate) and became a Seoulite.

Back to The North Korea

Life can play mysterious twists. In the early part of 1945, as a fourth grader, I alone was sent back to Cholwon, purportedly to seek safe refuge from the bombings by "enemy" planes, mainly B-29s. Since my parents chose to remain in Seoul, I was cut off from them when the country was split at the 38th Parallel in a flash as the WWII ended by the Japanese surrender. On August 15, 1945, on that unforgettable day of liberation, I too was a part of the utterly exuberant farmers of our village, who were running up and down the dirt roads, shouting and singing, occasionally looting some already empty houses, allegedly belonging to the Japanese or to their sympathizers. It was pure chaos. The mob scene, in retrospect, was a case of collective national catharsis which could not be corralled. As an aftermath of this excitement, I threw all the Japanese books I had (very few in reality) into the fire, an act I came to realize to be stupid and shortsighted. I did not know any better then. The initial excitement did not last long since Soviet troops were on the road and began disrupting the neighborhoods in earnest. Those unruly soldiers invited themselves to the village homes and often took house items at will. Young women had to be particularly careful not to be found when they approached homes. Meantime people were completely barred from crossing the border to the south.

Day by day, my situation became increasingly dire. I must go to Seoul, to my parents and to return to school. Finally, a plan was made. One day in December 1945, upon payment of a certain sum of commission, a smuggling scheme (if you can call it such) materialized. This time, accompanied by my paternal grandmother, I was loaded on a truck which had a burlap cover in the back. Light snow was falling, and our truck rumbled on bumpy roads until it was stopped by Soviet guards at a checkpoint. We were prewarned to lay low and stay still. We heard our driver calmly explaining that it was a local delivery of farm goods. Soldiers proceeded to the back of the truck for an inspection. That's when our driver quickly gunned the engine and sped away. Soldiers were shooting at us from behind, but we managed to make a safe escape. As a young boy, I felt more excited than scared. There were about 8 to 10 of us in the group and they were all adults. Not long after 'the escape,' we must have crossed the border because we were met this time by an American MPs. They were tall, clean clad, fair skinned, friendly, and smiling. It was my first encounter with Americans. Difference was like a night and day between Russians and Americans. This initial impression that Americans are good and benevolent, no matter how absurd it may sound today, remained with me for a long time. Count me as one lucky guy since very few Koreans in the north were able to flee to the south as easily or as early as I could.

6.25.1950.

Fateful day dawned with no warnings. I was 14 years old and was attending Gyeongdong Middle School as a second grader (8th grade). As the days moved on, we began to hear reports that North Korean troops attacked the South, but we also heard a government announcement that enemies were being repelled and we were successful in chasing them back to the north. Next day, we began to hear rumbling sounds of the distant cannons more frequently. People on the streets looked uneasy as some disturbing rumors began to fly. But victory will be ours after all, weren't we told? A government announcement continued, "Citizens! Stay calm. We are here with you. We will defend Seoul." By June 27th, people of Seoul started to move about in a frenzy, most of them with no sensible plans. Since we were living in Donamdong which lies in the foothill of Miari Hill, we thought we should move further away from their fronts. Rather laughably, we ended up spending a rainy night at a relative's home in Hyehwadong, which suffered minor damage that night from a cannon blast. Next morning, on June 28, we found endless columns of North Korean 'People's Liberation Army' soldiers marching through the streets of Seoul. They looked stern and somber, and moved on rather quietly. They did not display hostility or any other visible emotion to the people who lined up in the streets. Their uniforms were drab and some of them were carrying Soviet style machine guns and others with shoulder launchers. Huge tanks rumbled by but also oxcarts were being used to move materiel. Shabby looking military motorcycles sped ahead of troops, but they were not making as loud a noise as Harley Davidson could. Random corpses were strewn in their path, and nobody seemed to pay much attention. People were simply killed and abandoned in the name of war. Strange as it may sound on the street, many people already lined up cheering for the advancing North Korean soldiers, waving their flags in their hands. The meaning of this cruel picture proved to be a lasting vexation for the people and country. Carnage was not limited to the battle fields. Vengeful barbarism became rampant among citizens and countrymen for years to come. We belatedly found out the Han River bridge was detonated as the South Korean government and troops retreated from Seoul. We all became captives in the hostile city. Citizens of Seoul felt betrayed by their own government and lived with fear not knowing what horror awaits before the end of each day. Young people were systematically hunted, captured, and forcefully enrolled in the 'People's Militia,' and most remaining others were enlisted to carry out various functions. Not to be labeled 'Reactionary Element,' we all must show our devotion to General Kim Il-sung and adhere to the Communist teachings. Men had to join 'People's Council,' women to 'Women's Union,' younger man 'Democratic Youth Association' and students 'Democratic Student Association. etc.' I went to those 'brainwash' meetings and learned many patriotic songs. I found the Red Flag Song most moving and terrifying. Of course, many, fearing persecution, sought various hiding places as refuges. My 25-year-old uncle, a railway security guard, spent whole 3 months hidden in a hastily dug hole in our basement. The real morbidly tragic story about this uncle is that on September 27th, when the streets were quiet and North Korean soldiers were retreating, he came out to the street to celebrate the long awaited 'liberation' from captivity. He never came back and was later found killed and buried on the roadside, not far from where we lived. Multiple victims were found in that dirt pile, all killed with bamboo bayonets. On the other hand, another uncle, a police detective, survived because he did not go outside prematurely.

One day, my mother went to a 'Women's Union' meeting, with my younger brother, who was barely a year old, on her back. She was told that she should sacrifice the baby if he hinders her efficiency at work for the cause of revolution. Listening to the story, I physically shuddered. That narrative, 'you should kill your son if he hinders the cause of revolution' still reverberate with me and formed an unshakable belief that practice of the communist doctrine is downright evil. Occasionally we were called to come to the school for meetings. Once, while milling around the school yard, I heard screams of pain coming from one corner of the building. I was told that some of our teachers were captured and being tortured by a certain group of 'communist students.' Included among the tortured, according to the whisper, was the teacher who taught civics to our class.

One day, we were asked to come to the school. Then we were herded to the auditorium that morning. I believe that about 150 students were gathered there. No sooner did we enter the auditorium than the doors were shut closed. Then, one well-built young man appeared on the platform. We were told that he was a student from Kim Il-Sung University. He made an urgent impassioned speech on why we all should join 'People's Militia' to crush enemies, Americans, and its puppet government, the South Korea. When the speech was over, they herded all the students to prearranged trucks and took them away. Just like that. The whole thing was completed so swiftly. They never had time to say goodbye to their families. Out of 150 or so attended, they spared two smallest boys, so young deemed too small to be unfit for the combat mission as such. Instead, they took them to another place for some other use. I was one of those two undersized boys. We two were transported to the YMCA building in Chong-Ro 1 Ga. The people who transported us to this massive dark building quickly left the building without giving a word to us. All the doors to the outside were locked. The whole place, inside of the building, remained pitch dark even in the broad daylight. From many rooms, upstairs and downstairs, we heard shouts, groans, screams apparently from ongoing tortures. The whole building was used for the purpose of torture. I gathered we two small boys were brought in to do some menial chores, but thankfully nobody seemed to have noticed our presence. We remained hushed, and scurried around like two small, scared mice. Night was particularly dark and eerie, and groaning sounds and mourning sounds continued throughout the night. We were tired and hungry but also were too scared to look for any food around. Early in the morning, surreptitiously, we again checked if there was any door or backdoor to outside. Miraculously, at last, we found one front door kept unlocked. We escaped through the door, undetected. I started walking east and then north toward Donamdong. I collapsed on the street after passing Hyehwadong. I did not know how long I lost consciousness. When I woke up, I found myself being driven in an oxcart not far from Donamdong station. I don't remember whether I properly thanked the kindly man who must have picked me up from the street. The other 'lucky small boy' who survived the ordeal with me that night happened to be Lee Gwang-joon, who later graduated from Seoul National University Medical School, one year ahead of me, and currently is residing in Windsor, Canada. He is an MD but also worked as a Christian minister in later years. Being 'small' thankfully saved my life, but the anger and sadness resurface whenever I think about those innocent young boys taken away from their family, on that brief savage moment.

Then, there was another heartbreaking incident. One sunny day, I was walking on the street of our neighborhood with my best friend, Kim In-Young. We were in the same school and same class. He was born a few months earlier but about two inches taller than I was. We were stopped by some sort of communist party people who came out from nowhere. Apparently, they were out looking for any able bodies to snatch to replenish their manpower. They just looked at both of us and took my friend away, without any explanation. I was left out; it must be because I was too small for their purpose. My friend was a handsome young boy, particularly gentle and kindhearted. He lived alone with his elderly widowed mother. It was the most agonizing experience for me to tell her how her only son was kidnapped and taken away when I went home. We both cried. Her heartbreaking mournful wail never stopped. No one ever heard of his whereabouts since.

January 4 (1951) Retreat

With the news of the Million Chinese Human Wave offensive and retreat of our forces, we reflectively feared the impending occupation of Seoul again, this time by Chinese/North Korean forces. We joined the masses of fleeing refugees to the south. While many of peoples of Seoul chose Busan as their destination, somehow my family ended up in a small farming hamlet located 30 ri (ca. 7.5miles) south of Cheonan (Choong Nam province). The place was called Yong-mun, Gwakgoji, and Gees were the most prominent family. They had the largest share of lands in the area, and many villagers were related to them and/or work for them under their general guidance. Gees were known to be fair and generous to villagers. Probably the best-known Gee to us was Dr. Gee, Chang-yul, Professor of Physics at Seoul National University, who taught Physics to our class during our Premedical years. But the village was remote and isolated. Most villagers were uneducated and farmers. There was only one small elementary school, but no middle school or high schools nearby. While waiting for the war to end and return to Seoul, I ended up missing one whole year of school. Since I had no plan to remain as a farmer or village laborer, I could not wait any longer. I enrolled in Yeong-sung Middle School, about fifteen miles away from the village where we were. It was in the city of Cheonan and every morning I had to leave home before 5:00AM to get to school in time. Fifteen miles of daily walking through some winding and hilly dirt road was a unique experience. There was a river in the midpoint which we must cross to go to school. When the flimsy wooden bridge gets swept away by the flood, we had to turn back home. Once we had to repeat those wasted trips two days in a row. When we returned to school on the third day, our teacher chose not to believe our story and about 10 of us had to endure the harsh punishment with a baseball bat to our derrière. I thought it was barbaric and unfair, but it was before the time of demanding fairness was allowed. Oh, the school building itself was in pitiful shape, thanks to the artillery shells. We often sat on the ground (or on a piece of brick) during the class and the portable blackboard was regularly blown away on windy days. Unable to return to Seoul, upon graduating from middle school, I enrolled in Cheonan Engineering High School as freshman. Not that I had any wishes to become an engineer, but there were at that time only two high schools in Cheonan that I could choose from. One was the Agricultural High and the other was Engineering High. Most students were from farming families and preferred to enter Agricultural High. Since it did not matter to me, I chose engineering. Most of my fellow classmates were older and some were already married. Since they had to help with family farming chores after school, many dozed off during the class. I was one of few 'alien' students, meaning from the rank of refugees. School largely ignored me, even though I liked a few teachers, who themselves were 'refugees" from Seoul. When I was not in school, I hung around with village boys and volunteered to help them out in labor. It was a fond memory joining their minor mischiefs, such as stealing potatoes (often from their own lots) at night. Since my father was in Busan to earn the living for the family, I was given the role of "man of the house."

Frustration in the school front continued but we could not return to Seoul yet. Finally, my father decided not to wait any longer and chose to move to Inchon, closer to Seoul, if not quite Seoul. That's how I ended up graduating from Inchon high School. My parents moved back to Seoul as soon as they could. But I chose to remain in Inchon to finish my high school education. I was again dubbed an 'alien' and repeatedly bullied by school gangs because I was not originally from the area. Once those hoodlums knocked me out unconscious near the cemetery. No doubt, the war was to blame, at least in part, for the widespread lawlessness and breakdown of social codes. My imagined revenge never materialized, and I skipped my own graduation ceremony fearing another assault.

Epilogue

As Kelly Clarkson's song says, "What doesn't kill you, makes stronger." Our generation suffered through childhood and formative years. Many did not survive, and many suffered dearly into their adult years. Some who went through serious personal tragedies never fully recovered from their consequences. At the same time, many overcame the misfortune and rose to make important contributions in shaping modern Korea to its amazing height.

Many of my close relatives have perished. The place they (including my grandparents) lived was a vicinity of White Horse Highland (Baekma Goji), famous for the fiercest battles between the incomparable 9th Division of South Korean Army (White Horse Division) and Chinese Army and it was literally decimated into a wasteland. Everything was levelled and gone, and the graves of my most beloved ones could not be found. During five years of my service in Korean Army, my tour included one year of duty at the 9th Army (White Horse) Division as a medical officer.

After going through seven elementary schools and four middle and high schools, I was able to settle in only one college. I worked for 53 years at The University at Buffalo School of Medicine as a psychiatrist before retirement. Who says people never change?

6-Year-Old Boy and the Korean War

Dr. Paul Pyung Sung

In April 1950 I turned 6 years of age. The place where I was born and lived was a small old village near the 38th parallel in Korea, then place called Nulnori, Paju-gun, Kyonggi-do. My father was a reserved person, but he owned quite a lot of large parcels of land that he inherited as the land had been passed from generation to generation. We lived in a very large traditional Korean house, that was comparable to a large mansion of the west. The house had 99 rooms. While my father was reserved my mother was more open and outgoing in personality. Some said my mother was dynamic in personality, that was somewhat contrary to what old Korean society expected from the ladies of the home; to be gentle and less outgoing. I had two younger sisters.

In April 1950, the first elementary school was established, converted from the traditional Korean private school of the Chosen Dynasty, owned by my family. The Ministry of Education sent teachers to teach Hangeul (the Korean Language) to the people of the neighborhood for the first time, both children and adults. I was admitted to the school, and I was the youngest. But all the children of the school were put in one classroom in the beginning. I attended the school faithfully everyday regardless of what we were taught.

There was a small garden behind our house, a stream flowing in front of it, many thatched houses were gathered, and rice fields and open fields were spread out, and there was a small ditch between them. As early summer drew near, many flowers bloomed and withered, and it was a peaceful rural village where there were no quarrels or greed, where the farmers, the tenant farmers, worked hard to plow and sow my family's rice fields.

On June 25, the North Korean regime, Kim Il-sung, secretly prepared to invade the South and occupied the defenseless South Korea, occupying almost the entire peninsula within two months. Unprepared for the sudden occupation of my hometown by the northern communist forces, we hurriedly evacuated to a relative's house in the neighboring village. According to my mother, after the Communists took over the village, she asked 'where could the owner of that 99-room house hide? What else? The vicious landowner should be caught and shot to death right away.' It is said that all the people in the neighborhood defended my father as a good person who helped the poor by opening his granary for the needy. It is said that the communist party gave permission to contact such a good person to return to their homes and my father was expected to return home safely. From what I heard later that, when the Communist Party took over, the landowners and the rich were killed, and after the village was freed and democracy was restored, those who were active as Communist Party member were killed, so death was rife in every village. But it was said that there was no killing of each other in our village.

During the war, my father was most of time in bed like a very sick. He seems to have thought that by doing so he would be able to deal with the hardship, the stress of the war like, as though he was feigning. However, because he had been lying in bed so long, we did not pay attention to what was taking place. One day we thought he was not breathing. He was found to be dead. None in the family knew how sick he was or even sick at all. When my father's body left the house with simplified funeral procession, I knew I would never see him again, but I was so surprised by that I did not cry, in fact I couldn't even cry.

Now we have become a family of four. When the U.N. troops entered the war, and the North Korean communist force was pushed back to north by the U.N. forces occupying almost entire North Korean territory. No sooner allied force reached the northern border of Korea, a large number of Chinese communist forces was sent and came into the war, pushing back the allied forces. The war started in the summer and the war is in the cold winter. The Chinese forces were so large that the U.N. forces had to retreat again by using variety of the tactics.

My family also fled to the south as the U.N. forces retreated. My mother carried my younger brother on her back and a large bag on her head. I had to carry the baby on my back. Over the mountain covered with white snow, I could see the dead Chinese soldiers scattered here and there in vast areas. Even looking at the dead body, I had no emotion in me. It was as though I thought that I couldn't afford to feel anything on the evacuation route. Our final refugee destination was South of the Han River, Yesan, Chungcheongnam-do. We know that it was the town where my surname originated. We hoped they would treat us like their own relatives. There were many of the same surnames living there.

Now spring has come again, the snow has melted, and the weather started to warm up. But we were still walking towards Yesan. My mother was carrying my younger brother (4 years old), a big bag on her head, and my other brother and the sister were struggling to follow my mother.

My mother, who found a place like a puddle, stopped, and tried to rest. She looked tired with the struggle of carrying all her children. She said, "it's too hard to go on like this" and then after a deep sigh, she said "let's leave your brother here!" I pushed my little sister on her back as though I was trying to stop my mother removing my sister from her back. I said with crying voice "I don't want you to do that, Mommy!" I kept repeating the same.

Years later, my mother told us the story a few times. How could I forget the story. I heard later that it was not uncommon for some family could not bring every member of their family, particularly the little ones, and ended up separating from each other. Some time I felt shivering chill when I remember the incidence and I imagined how I would have been able to deal with it if we left my baby sister there as my mother spitted out from her mouth. I could not stop crying. But it was not an uncommon story.

If my baby sister or my brother was left in the puddle, my family relationships would have collapsed, and I certainly believe that my family and I would not exist now.

When we finally arrived in Yesan, many of the same surname helped us in many ways, such as financially and so forth, as they say in the village that we should be treated like their family. It was truly warm greetings, as though we were their real relatives.

As my mother was visiting her customers as a pack peddler merchant from door to door, she describes her experience as follows. She realized the hardship of the merchant life. And, she had such remorse that she should have treated them better with more generosity when the merchants visited her in the past as she was regarded to be the rich lady of the large house.

I started attending the new school, an elementary school in the town. As it happened often during the war local children bullied the children of the refugee, I was also mistreated by local children. As a child it was too harsh for me, and I remembered this painful memory for a long time.

When the war stopped, I was nine-year-old, my family of four settled in Seoul at last. I was able to graduate from all the schools one by one, elementary, middle, and high school and college. I got married, and then My family came to United States.

While many people have given us hardship, mostly because of such issues as property ownership and so forth. But I am so grateful that many also helped us to face the problems and solve them. My mother also joined us in America. She lived happily until she left us at the age of 94 years old.

That little sister who survived by coming to the south on my back lives in Las Vegas. She is doing well, retiring from her successful vocation, and now living not too far from my home. My younger brother is retired too and lives not too far from me.

Now I am 78 years old, and after 40 years of working as a doctor, I have retired and live quietly in Fairfax, Virginia. I am very grateful to God for guiding me this far. Surviving from such fierce war, going through hardship as refugee, thinking about the Korean 6.25 War, I have nothing but gratitude.

The 6.25 Experience; A Story of a Naughty Boy

Two national anthems

Eungshik Won, PhD

On June 25, 1950, I was an elementary school student. My family was poor, but I had many brothers and sisters, so I grew up without the love and interest of my parents. In addition to that, I had three mothers: a big mom, my mom, and a little mom. As an illegitimate child, I grew up in difficult circumstances, but there was little interference from adults, and I roamed freely and had more experiences than other children.

It was about 70 years ago, so I can't remember it well, but I would like to summarize the events that remain in my memory. Wonju, Kangwon province, Korea where I was born, roads were parts of the road that came down from the North Korea when the People's Army invaded the South, and parts of the road that went up back when they withdrew from the south. And since the roads were going up when the Republic of Korea (ROK, south Korea) Army advanced north, I could see a lot of the North Korean People's Army and the ROK Army.

The 6.25 War

One day, when the sound of a cannon was suddenly heard from afar, my father hurried back home and told his family that we had to evacuate. My father told me and my younger sister Bang-sik to stay and keep the house, and my brother-in-law, Dong-sik, and Hang-sik to go with my father. The family packed their small bags and left the house to evacuate. I was going to follow too, but my father said to stay. If someone might set our house on fire, I must protect the house. My father left. Because there were so many families, my sister and I did not seem to care whether we lived or died.

My family evacuated and I did not eat anything all day because I didn't know how to cook. Fortunately, my neighbor's grandmother came to our kitchen and cooked rice and prepared side dishes for me, so I ate. There were a lot of potatoes in the kitchen storage. When the grandmother put the potatoes in the basket, peeled the skins, put them in the pot and then put them on fire, the potatoes are nicely cooked. We ate only potatoes for breakfast, lunch, and dinner. I didn't know how to make side dishes, so I dipped the potatoes in salt and ate them.

It had been about 4 days past, in the morning, I heard the gate of the house was broken by force, and when I went out, soldiers were rushing through the gate. There were about five of them, and one of the highest-ranking people asked where my parents were, and I said they had fled. "Now we take over this house, we are the People's Army who came to liberate south Korea." When he saw the picture of my eldest brother hanging on the wall of the floor, Daecheongmaru, he asked me who the person in the picture pointing at my brother's. I told him that he was my eldest brother. Four of the soldiers searched my house thoroughly and ordered subordinates to check the food supplies so that there is no problem with cooking dinner, lunch, and breakfast for themselves. And, the large adult bedroom, the closet, the small rooms, and the large floor were all taken for their use. My sister and I took a blanket from the storage and slept in the small room attached to the kitchen and stayed there.

The People's Army forcibly took over our house

The People's Army cooked rice, grilled meat, and made side dishes quite well. When it was time to eat, they called us over and gave us some cooked rice and even the meat. Two days after the People's Army came taking over my house, they said that the

People's Army welcome convention was held at the marketplace and leaving only two people on duty everyone was allowed, I should say ordered, to go to the marketplace for the welcome festival. I followed them along and they gave me permission. I quickly became familiar with the People's Army staying in my house, so only I followed them around.

Some unfortunate people like the fathers and the mothers of some of the friends of mine in the village were abused by the people's army at the welcome festival in front of the county office. They ordered to shout General Kim Il-sung for hurrahs. I thought I could understand why they abused poor people. They also seemed to understand their plight. Most of them were dog butchers, cow butchers, pig butchers, and thieves, who were ordinary and uneducated. The People's Army and the people of Wonju gathered quite a lot in front of the local county office. Everyone was acting excited and said the People's Army had liberated us! Shouting hurrah of General Kim Il-sung! It was a riotously shouting of large populace.

At that time, a soldier with a flashing badge of rank came out and raised a loudspeaker and announced that now that they have liberated Wonju County, everyone should be freed from the oppression of South Korea. They gave the People's Republic flag to people, and I got one too. Then they hurrahed for the People's Republic again and again. If I didn't follow it, I thought I'd get confused, so I followed.

Then, a well-dressed skinny man went up on the platform. A lot of people were watching. One of the high-ranking soldiers announced that since this person, who just went up to the podium, was elected to the chairman of the People's Committee and his words were the same as those of General Kim Il-sung. Then, he wrapped a red cloth around the man's left arm,

It was a dog butcher, called 'gae baek-jeong', the father of a close friend of mine whose job was butchering dogs under the bridge of the town and burning the dog's fur. His son happened to be a classmate of mine, so we were good friends and I got to know him well. Since this friend's father became the chairperson, the dog was butchered by someone else who came from another town in the north. This father of my close friend wearing a shabby suit with an epaulet on the left side of his shoulder is still vivid in my memory even now.

Fortunately, it was rumored that he did not commit any atrocities or evil deeds such as harassing people. It was possible that he might have served as chairman by taking the side of the people and caring for them. When Wonju was recaptured by the allies, and now the former chairman of the People's Committee said he was going to be killed for sure, but the town folks all said that we were helped by him and was not an evil doer.

I thought it was fortunate. I came to think that people can survive if they are good and helpful under such unavoidable situation in which a man might be forced to do the things evil. After the welcome ceremony, we had lunch. To prepare the lunch for a large number of people of the town, when we butchered many cows and pigs, and the smell of cooking the butchered animals vibrated in whole town. Everyone in the town was satisfied.

It reminded me of the way I was alone at home earlier, so I asked for another bowl, thinking about my younger brother waiting at home and they gave it to me. I brought home the bowl of meat soup excitedly. I was so happy watching Bang-sik, the young brother, eating breathlessly the whole bowl of meat soup. I could not hold back the tears from my eyes with the thought of how hungry he would have been if he did not have the bowl of soup.

There were two of North Korean People's Army in my house. One day, I could not see the younger one. He was a little bit taller than I was. I remembered what he said. He could catch sparrows in the backyard. When I went there looking for him. Indeed, I saw him trying to catch birds with a slingshot (rubber band gun).

He caught about 7-8 sparrows already. He stripped sparrows' feathers and plumes and grilled them over a charcoal fire. After that, whenever I had times, I asked him 'Hey little comrade!' and asked him to catch the birds.

When I asked the age of the little People's Army, he said he was 16. From then on, I followed him at every opportunity. After the People's Army was in my house, I felt comfortable because I was allowed to eat what they ate. According to them, since they came to liberate south Korea, one of the high-ranking officers gave speeches in the mornings and evenings that they should be kind to the people of the South. I was allowed to get in and out of their offices or quarters without hesitation.

As they said, the People's Army who first marched did not commit any evil deeds. But I don't know how abused I must have been if I thought I was political or what they called a reactionary. I couldn't understand their atrocities without reason. What and how could a 12-year-old boy know?

One of my friends in the neighborhood asked me to go to school with him as the school was opening the following day. So, I asked the old lady next door to give me a hand by taking care of my young sister. The next day, I was able to go to school with my friends.

When I went to the classroom, there were three large pictures hanging on the wall. It was a picture of Kim Il-sung, Mao Zedong, and Stalin. The teacher was also a new one the first time we met. What about General Kim Il-sung, what about Mao Zedong, and what about Stalin, everyone said that they sent troops to the south to liberate south Korea. From the first day, when one enters the classroom, you have to greet the three people at a 90° angle bow. 'Hurray! General Kim Il-sung! Hurray! President Mao Zedong! Hurray! Marshal Stalin!' We were told to call out loudly 3 times. Then he said that he would teach us the national anthem, so we said that we all know the national anthem well. He said the national anthem we knew was the wrong one. Even as a child, I thought that something was wrong. 'Blood stains on the stem of Chang-baik Mountain, blah blah blah...' Before 6.25, there were about 60 students in our class, but after the People's Army came in, there were only 15 students in our class. Most of them left the town taking refuge, evacuating the town, some children were not allowed to come to school by their parents, but the teacher told us to bring all our close friends to school. At the same time, the teacher gave me a notebook and a pencil, saying that it was a gift that General Kim Il-sung gave to children in South Korea.

People's Army retreat

When I was in the 5th grade of elementary school, during the Korean War, a close friend of mine came and asked me to go to school the next day. I said I didn't want to go to the people's army school, but he said that if I go to school, they'll give me a lot of presents. Only 5th and 6th graders were asked to come to school. The next day, I went to school with my friends, and something seemed wrong. The 5th graders were asked to stand in this row and the 6th graders were told to stand in that row. However, there were quite a few people's army soldiers around the children with pistols in their hands on their shoulders.

Then, one by one, they called each other and told us to carry the backpack. It was very heavy. Some students did not come to school that day, and there were about 12 students in grades 5-6. Since everyone is carrying a backpack on their shoulders, from now on, we too have become the shining People's Republic of the People's Army. I had no choice but to follow the directions. I was told to go pass the Sinda-rae Pond and over the Chiak-san Mountain, and I almost thought I was going to die.

Hundreds of the People's Army crossed Chiak-san Mountain and marched toward Gang-rim. Suddenly, a plane named Sacksacki (allied jet fighters) approached and fired bullets, causing several people to run out and crouch. The People's Army was lying in the ditch and could not get up. Thinking quietly and thinking that this was an opportunity, I shouted to my friends to throw off their luggage and escape towards the mountain. Then we took off our luggage and ran away. The northern soldiers accompanied us earlier began to shoot at us with their pistols, but we kept running away from there. The People's Army, lying down in the ditch, kept shooting the children with their pistol.

6.25 war and mortar shells

On that road, I was told to run away in a hurry, and after crossing Mt. Chi-ak, I looked back and only four of the boys in my class followed me. After taking a break by the Sinda-re Pond, I asked if anyone knew what happened to us, and one of the boys said that what we carried was a mortar shell. I don't know how many, but they were very heavy. I found out after a while that it was the line of the People's Army withdrawing back to the north and we were ordered to follow. Everyone crossed Mt. Chi-ak, passed through Gang-rim, An-heung, and Jinbu, and continued to the Tae-baek Mountains to go north Korea.

I rushed towards the mountain. The moment we crossed the mountain, we encountered the People's Army. At that moment, I thought I was dead. At that same time a plane suddenly flew over, and as it flew toward the valley, it fired a barrage of machine guns without mercy. I could not tell if and how many were killed or injured. The People's Army that they encountered quickly ran into a cave, an abandoned mine on the mountainside. It seemed that there were about 15-20 people there. One of them motioned towards us and beckoned us to enter the cave. Pretending not to be seen and crossing the ridge, we ran away with all our breath.

Seven North Korean People's Army captured

As I was coming down from the hilltop, several soldiers with black paint on their faces appeared. The tough looking people like a goblin shouted, "Raise your hands!" They pointed the gun at my chest, and my heart was pounding. I raised my hand. And when I looked closely, they were not the People's Army, but South Korean National Army. "It was so nice to see you, officer!" I explained that we did nothing wrong, but the People's Army took us over as porters. The soldier with the captain's badge on his helmet seemed to be the company commander. So, when I said that it was the way to escape now, they asked where we live, so I told them that we live in Wonju. And, when the Armed Forces of the South was about to cross the mountain, "Are you going to catch the Northern People's Army now?" I asked. They looked at me and smiled softly and said 'yes.' After a flash of thought, I said to the leader "Officer! please come here!" and he motioned for me and then came close to me. I told the officer that over this pass, there was a large cave on the right side, and I told them that I saw a lot of northern people's soldiers entering there. He then asked me about it in detail. The man looked very tense. A senior sergeant and a few soldiers gathered, then they seemed to discuss a strategy of sort. How to go over that side over the pass and approached the cave. A soldier came with a portable megaphone. The captain shouted into the megaphone. "If you resist, everyone will be killed." And then "Everyone raise your hands and surrender," he shouted through the horn.

There was no sign in the cave. I wondered if the People's Armies had left the cave and fled. The captain kept shouting, and the soldiers surrounded the cave and aimed their guns. It must have been about 30 minutes passed. From the side of the cave, the People's Army hung a white cloth on a stick and crawled out of the cave. "Raise your hand and come out!" The captain shouted, "we're not going to shoot because you are prisoners of war." From there, one by one, raising their hands, came out of the cave. There were seven people. It was the people's army looking back at us. He didn't say anything. The captain gave us a box of biscuits, he looked at us with satisfaction and said that we did a good job. I was very hungry, so I shared the biscuits with my friends. Of course, we thought it was a nice gesture for our help for the brief war time situation.

North Korean Army

One day, when they occupied my home, the People's Army had a big lunch, so I ate with them. I think it was around 2pm then. There was a guard standing next to the gate of my house, dozing off behind the gate. I opened the gate and went out. Very that moment an American jeep flew to the side of the main road in front of my house, where the Moon-mak was flapping the Taegeukgi, the flag of South Korea. How did he know? A truck belonging to the allied troop arrived, loaded with soldiers. When the guard of North Korean saw something like this, he fell in shock. What possibly could he do? Everyone else was taking a nap as they all had a big lunch a little earlier. This guard finally made the decision and shouted at the top of his voice. Only word came out of his mouth was "Emergency!"

When the National Defense Forces of Republic of Korea had invaded this town, the back wall of my house was fenced with boards. There were the northern soldiers who couldn't lose bags or backpacks tags on their bodies and could not even wear shoes as they couldn't find one belonging to each of them as the situation became chaotic. Even there were man who were still wearing his sleeping in pants only. All of them ran into the field behind our house.

While the northern troops were in chaos, there were loud sounds of the front gate being opened. Obviously, it was hit by many rifles at the same time in unison. At last, there was the sound of the door breaking down. A group of young soldiers with faces painted in black came in. They looked at me and asked where the People's Army had gone. I told them that they had run away over there pointing a direction, that pointing was to the field. It was a lot of fun for me as I was following the South Korean soldiers.

As the People's Army fled, some of them set fire to the supply warehouse. There was a school called Hakseong National School, not far from my home. I did remember that the northern troop used it as their supply depot. They piled up rice high mountainously, but now it was set on fire as they were running away. Later, my family suggested the burnt rice might be edible and so I went there to try by eating some burnt rice and I got a stomachache, and anyone who took the burnt rice all suffered stomachache for a few more days.

When I went to the field behind our house, it seemed that the corpses of the People's Army were over a hundred. One of them had his pistol on his shoulder, and the other was shot upside down in his ditch, and when I looked closely, he had a watch on his right arm. Also, his feet looked up at the sky and his shoes still looked good. When I untied the laces and tried on the shoes, the size was a little too big for me, but they were comfortable to wear.

I took off all the watches and put them on my wrist. As I turned around, there was a horse, so I grabbed the reins of the horse and pulled it out. I brought two of them and tied the reins on a peach tree in the backyard. I called my naughty friends in the neighborhood, and I heard from him that the People's Army had watches, shoes, emergency food, etc., and he took as many as he could. I let him bring them all so that we could compare. Whatever one might be thinking about the behaviors it was just irresistible for us to do that as we had never seen those so called

'Emergency things' until then. You cannot stop the curiosity of the boys of my age.

When the South Korean national army was gone, we decided that we should play soldier with that pistol later, and we brought it under the floor of our house and kept it. The grandmother next door looked at it and giggled. The grandmother told a soldier (National Defense Force of South) about it. When the soldiers came, the boys had to give them all away, but the soldiers gave up some items, such as watches, emergency food, shoes, etc. The horses were dragged by soldiers, too. I looked for a little comrade in the pile of corpses, but there was none. I don't know whether he died or if he's alive, but if he's alive, I'd like to meet him.

Wounded by a pistol

We descended the mountain and came down to Sindare Pond. But my shoes were sticky. I didn't realize I was shot, but there was blood on one of my feet. I sat on the edge of the reservoir and saw that a bullet had pierced the left side of my body. There was a lot of blood on my clothes. I still have that wound. All five of our children managed to escape, and three of us were shot and killed in the valley beyond Mt. Chi-ak. When the people who lived near the reservoir saw that I was injured, they put an unknown medicine on my wound and gave me rice and potatoes to satisfy my hunger, as it appeared to be obvious.

Upon entering the city, on the way home, my younger sibling Bang-sik was sleeping on the floor all by herself. Oh! my poor little sister, my tears were about to come out, but the grandmother next door came. She said that Bang-sik ate a lot, so she should be fine. After showing the scar on my side, the grandmother mashed up cooked potatoes and applied it to the hole in my side. I still have scars on my side.

I thought I had done well telling the captain that there were People's Armies in the cave but thinking about the three dead close friends made my heart ache. One of them was in my class and was a soccer player.

I went to the kitchen to find something to eat, there was rice and boiled fish. I ate and slept. When I woke up in the morning, the women of the women's union in the neighborhood came to my house, making rice cake, called songpyeon and pork. It was nice. Today is Chuseok and we will eat rice cakes and pork.

Allied Forces Successfully Landed in Incheon

As the Allied Forces successfully recaptured Seoul as the Incheon Landing Operation was successful, the supply routes for all the People's Army that had advanced to the Nakdonggang Front were cut off, and many of the People's Army were retained in the south and became prisoners of war. Since there was no way to escape through the central frontline of the war, they had to go beyond Chi-ak Mountain in Wonju, Gangwon Province, toward Oraesan Mountain, and had to choose the Taebaek Mountains to retreat. If we had been called out there, we would have been dragged to the north. It should have been dying helplessly without choices this way or dying that way. I was so preoccupied with the thought that I had to go home quickly because my younger sister was waiting at home. So, I have chosen to escape betting with my life.

At the same time, I thought that it was a good thing that we had escaped in the wind and rain. We had no idea what happened to the 7 POWs. I imagined that they would have been living somewhere in South Korea in search of freedom after released from the POW camps in Geo-je Island. My brother-in-law, Baek Seong-geun, was also released from the Non-san Prison Camp as a prisoner of war, I learned late on. The management team of Jinro Soju Company were all from Jinnampo, who came from North Korea. My brother-in-law was also a close friend of some of them because they lived in the same neighborhood. Thanks to that opportunity, after I became an adult, I got a job at the Jinro company and My brother-in-law also got a job at the Jinro company, which became the foundation for my life in Seoul. It was truly an amazing relationship. After a while, he and I went to Nonsan, Chungcheongnam-do. He went into a thatched house in a village and found the owner who said that there was someone else living there. My brother-in-law returned to Seoul after a few days with a disappointed expression. My brother-in-law seems to have tried to own the house if there is no owner. At that time, there were many unoccupied houses or land. This is because many people died on the way or were taken away by the People's Army and never returned.

6.25 War People's Army retreat

For a few days, I took my friends from the neighborhood and began to search for the field where the People's Army was fleeing. It was like a ditch, and I searched through piles of corpses and collected watches, emergency food, backpacks, shoes, etc. It was fun at the time. Suddenly, I thought it would be fun to play soldier-game with boys, so I told my friend to take a hat from the corpses of the People's Army and put them on and played the game with them.

A friend who lives next door was grunting and pulling something in the ditch that he had found. It turned out to be a corpse wearing a helmet. There was a sign of the rank of sergeant in the helmet. This friend said that he was going to serve in the national army and should wear a helmet, but his head was too small. It was ridiculous look that the helmet covered his whole face. Everyone laughed and laughed.

On the way, I went to the cemetery behind Haemang-chon. When they were playing a soldier-game, everyone was wearing the People's Army hat and only one of them was wearing a helmet. We were running and running and had fun. Then, suddenly, one of the boys pulled the trigger of a pistol. Everyone was scared, so we fell on the ground and looked at the friend, and the friend's face went white in surprise. The sound of the gunshot was loud, so it could be heard in the distance, so after a while, three young men went to security officers to tell the story of gun shotes and two soldiers followed. We were told to put all the guns on the ground. As the soldiers carried three guns, they told them not to do this from now on. Heck, 12-year-old and 13-year-old boys know what they're all about.

Family Returns

All the People's Army fled from the house leaving only two people left in the big house, the residents. During Chuseok season arrived, the grandmother of my next door made a lot of rice cakes and pancakes and cooked the rice. I ate them for a few days to my satisfaction. One night, while I was sleeping in the large room, someone shook me to wake me up. When I opened my eyes, my father was standing there. His face turned dark and at first glance he looked like a bandit. When I got up and sat down, I could tell he was my father. He said to me, "you go to your aunt's house tomorrow and asked Hang-sik and your brother-in-law to come back here." I don't remember if one of my brothers, Dongsik, was there. After finishing my breakfast, I crossed Mt. Chi-ak, crossed the river, and then arrived at the small town of An-gol by the evening.

When I went into my aunt's house, my aunt recognized me after asking a few questions and then she held my hands and started crying. I slept for the night and by crossing Mt. Chi-ak I returned home.

When I went to school a few days later I found there were quite a few in my class. When I told some of my close friends about playing with soldiers-game and running away from the People's Army, and so on, everyone was surprised. But I could not help but laugh and I laughed again and again.

I went to school without a notebook or pencil. The next day, from the moment I stepped into the school, I had a question in my mind. I was wondering if the Chairman of the People's Army committee was dead or ran away. So, I asked to his son, one of the classmates and friend of mine, "Is your father dead or alive?" He said he was alive.

My mother passed away. My father was in a situation where he would attend his business every few days. I had a supply of pencils and notebooks, but I could not tell anyone where I got them. One day, my father came home. I was happy to have the chance to ask my father for some money. What do you use it for? He asked. I need to buy a notebook and a pencil, I said. He gave me a 10 won bill. I was so grateful and happy, because I thought the only person in the world who gave me money was only my father. The money was crumpled, and I even unfolded the crumpled money with iron to make the paper money looked like new one.

One day when I came home from school, I had to go through the Wonju train station before reaching my home. In the yard of the train station, there was a man selling candy, even big candy canes. I was praying for a couple of days that I would like to buy and eat that eyeball-candy. It's been about 3 weeks since I got the money from my father. After I came home and took out the money one day. I even ironed it. I decided that I was going to try a candy cane, and I ran to the station at Wonju Station happily.

I gave him 10 won, asking "please give me some eyeball-candy or candy cane." Surprisingly, he gave me the money back. I asked him why. He told me that he could not use that money I handed to him because of the currency reform that was taking place. But I said I want to try candy anyway. He gave me one for free. I put the candy in my mouth. The taste was amazing for the first time in my life.

From then on, I was angry at my father as though he made a fool out of me with the useless money. Then my father came home one day, so I spoke about it. He laughed and laughed saying nothing. However, one day, a mischievous man came in through the gate of my home making the cranking noise with the pair of metal scissors. I went out of the room to find my brother. Un-sik brother suddenly turned into a pumpkin candy man (hobak yut jangsa). When he saw me, he pretended to be happy and said to bring rubber shoes, metal fittings, and so to change with the candy. I told him to wait. Then I went to my sister-in-law's house, there was no one there, so I brought a pair of rubber shoes and a brass washbasin. We got the candy by exchanging with the things I brought from home. I shared the candy with Un-sik. Ban-sik and Changsik. They all enjoyed the so called hobak-yut (Pumpkin candy).

One day, I was going to the creek with the children of the neighbor to catch loach and crucian carp, and there were tomatoes and melons in the middle of the field too. We picked some tomatoes and melons without permission from the owner. We enjoyed them very much anyways. Was it an enjoyable life in the middle of such a hardship?

The People's Chairman becomes a dog butcher again.

After some time, I was curious about Chairman, the dog butcher, so I went to his home on my way home from school. He became a dog butcher again. One of my friends told me he wanted to give me something and what he gave me was skinny meat like a stick. What is this? I asked. It is good for man and expensive, he said. While I was eating it, he made a bowl of soup with a lot of meat. It was delicious. After that, if I wanted to eat the soup, I would go to this friend's house and sit on the floor, he would give me the delicious soup. But he asked me never to mention his father's name alluding his job as the people's chairman in the past during the communist occupation.

1.4 Retreat Evacuation Route

One day, as the South Korean army was retreating, everyone said that they had to evacuate again too. It was snowing and cold. I was worried about where I had to go, and whether I should stay in my house to watch it or not. But this time, everyone said we all should go together, leave the town. Dong-sik, the older brother, was evacuated by the help of the father of his friend because he was in a high position at the Wonju police station. Do-shik was brought to my house saying that he was my older brother, so my family and I walked towards Mun-mak on the way of the evacuation route together.

After walking for a while, I noticed that there was a small village and when I entered, there were a lot of people. Every room was full. My brother told me to go to that paddy field and bring the straw as much as I could. I took the straw bale 2-3 times and laid it on the floor of the barn.

Then I went to the main room of the house, thinking that I should have a blanket. I saw a little girl on the floor sleeping, and there was a blanket in the corner of the room. I went for the second time and the girl woke up and was crying while her mother was not saying anything. I found that she couldn't walk, and she was crawling around in the room. She had a washbasin full of rice and water in a bucket. It looked like the mother was trying to feed the child to survive even though she was gone. It is unbelievable how can a child stay at home alone. When I think about the situation my heart was very painful.

How could she leave her baby like that? Then, there was more bad news heard from the refugees. U.S. soldiers come to this side of the gate, and they said soldiers were cannibals and eat the people unconditionally when they see them. All said 'we were all scared and should leave here early in the morning before the American cannibals arrived.

Crossing the Frozen Chungju Dal-Lae River

As the large family were heading towards Chung-ju, the little boy in the house left behind. We arrived at Mok-gye of the Chung-ju River on foot by the afternoon. The river was frozen, so it was easy to cross. But suddenly, something slammed onto the ice plate, and I fell, and when I looked around, a large cow fell and couldn't stand up. Numbers of men tried but couldn't even get it up. So, one young man shouted, telling the owner of the cow to either slaughter the cow or leave it alone.

I stood still and looked around, but the cow only blinked its eyes. The owner asked how to slaughter the cow. The young man said he could do it because he was a butcher for his living. So, the owner nodded his head as well. The young man hit the cow with a big stone on the forehead, but it didn't budge. Hitting the head with a large stone 3-4 times he killed the cow at last. When he asked if anybody had a kitchen knife, people presented various knives, mostly were kitchen knives. The young man said that he had butchered cattle in Chung-ju, and then he simply settled the cattle.

People who wanted to eat share of the meat lined up, so I was allowed to stand in the line near the first because I was a kid and Doo-Shik brother was allowed to stand next to me. The young man gave a large chunk of the meat to me, and Doo-Shik brother also got a chunk of meat. There were a lot of empty houses along the riverbank, so anyone could go in them, so we went into one of the big houses, and even my older brother occupied one of the empty houses.

Doo-shik, my brother and I went to the hill to gather tree branches every morning. One day I was going to the hill to get tree branches, and I saw a nice, tiled house on the hillside. I checked if anyone was in the house. I searched the house thoroughly, there were a lot of soybeans, and there were so many beans in several big jars. I got a gunny sack and carried the soybeans to my home. It was quite a lot of soybeans. Everyone was surprised, and there was a lot of fuss among family about it. My eldest aunt (Yu Chang's mom) liked it the most. From then on, I ate soybean porridge and soup; the cheong-guk-jang, like a miso soup every day. I thought there might be more beans. I went there again the next day with Doo-Shik brother. We found a large room, there was a picture of the Buddha and some figures of something like monsters. I thought initially that this was a temple. I was going to take only beans. I opened every big jar, but there was no rice. For a while, we had a good time eating to our fullest, thanks to beans. I brought some rice from Munmak as emergency food. My father said that he should go to Wonju with me the following day. The next day, my sister-in-law made rice cakes called injeol-mi for us and I left with my father, and of course I carried the food.

After walking all day long, we reached the foot of a high mountain, and my father said that we should be able to cross the mountain, meaning we could climb the mountain. We had lunch when we reached the top of the mountain at last. We saw many dead human bodies along the way. Surprisingly, when I looked closely, they were either the corpses of the People's Army of North or the allied soldiers. They were all over the place.

When I went to the ditch and found my father who was also amazed by the sheer number of corpses of soldiers. He said, "That's the People's Army and this is not the National Defense Army." He must be trying to say most of the dead were the soldiers of the North.

Drinking Rotten Liquid of Corpses

No matter how hard I looked for the water to drink, I couldn't find it. In fact, my father's face turned white. I crossed the hill and came to the foot of the mountain. I found a stream; I sat down in a ditch and near the stream I drank the water of the stream until I was satisfied. We were shocked when we realized that the water was rotten as it washed the corpses. When I realized it I felt sick and threw up all the food I ate earlier.

We arrived at Moori-sil at around sunset. My father went to the thatched house on the corner of the mountain. The house was empty. We decided to sleep there overnight. The next day, my father stopped at a house in the Hakseong-dong. He said he knew the owner. After having something for breakfast early in the morning, we continued to move along the stream. My home was not far away. When we arrived where my house used to stand, the house was gone. It must be bombed, I thought. I turned around and went to the place where the soldiers were playing in the back yard of the Haemang Village, and I saw the big house. The house was fine, but dozens of local dogs gathered there fighting for the bones of animals. We sat down on the floor of the big house, and the dogs started to bark loudly for a long time.

Suddenly, there was voice of a man, saying he wanted to come out from the closet. I approached the closet of the main room. An old man with a dark face in dirty clothes like a bagger appeared. He came down from the closet and looked at me. He sounded as though he was surprised. He said loudly "brother!" He started asking me what happened to me, where I was and so forth. I briefly told him about it all. So, my family is all near the Chungju River, and my father was hiding in the Moori-sil. Before the 6.25 war, there were times when I was teased with jokes that I was the son of a concubine, but now it was heartbreaking to see them hugging me and making me happy.

Meeting with older brother

Then he told me to take his backpack and bring it to my father. He told me he is serving the Reconnaissance Team, which is the advance team of the ROK Army. He asked me to tell my family that he was doing well. After a while, I took his backpack and walked to the back road towards the mountain safely to my family. When I entered the room, my father was sleeping. When he got up, he was very pleased. As I talked responding so I saw the tears forming in his eyes.

When I opened the backpack, there was quite a lot of money in it. There were also several cans of meat and a few cartons of American cigarettes, which my father loved. The next morning, we had breakfast early and went toward my home in Chungju. When I arrived at my home, there was no one. I shouted hoping someone might hear me. I called the name of the older aunt of mine as I was hoping she might be around.

Suddenly a voice was heard from the inside of the room, and when the closet door was opened, every one of my relatives who lived there was there hiding in the closet. I asked them to come down. They all came down, and I was puzzled and so was my father as all the ladies covered their faces with something very dark, like charcoal. I thought they were in the shape of a goblin. They explained that there was a rumor that the Americans would come and catch all women they find. There was also a black person among the American troops. The ladies were hiding in the closet to hide from them.

I looked around the house for my cousins. But when something crawled out of the corn heap on the corn stalk in the middle of the field, it was my cousin I was looking for. He was hiding there motionless when I saw him, and I was scared. The airplanes of the allied forces flew in every day. The American bombers came and bombed every day, The whole town became a wasteland. Everyone suddenly became beggars for a living. Only the Wondong Catholic Church in Wonju stood tall as an undamaged building. The uncountable number of American soldiers came to Wonju at a time when many people of the Wonju were struggling to find food. If there was an empty space, US troops set up tents for their station.

There was a large trash container next to the US military base mostly, and they threw their leftovers into the large trash container. The people of the town picked up the food by scooping buckets. They prepared various ways to eat. There were many things that I had never seen before, such as sausages, bread, bacon, butter, jam and so forth. They put all those mixed in liquid cooking like soups. This was called 'budaejjigae', meaning the soup of troops, a kind of soup that Koreans talk about quite often since. Everyone said it tasted good. Also, when we go near the US military base, often the soldiers throw things like something edible and useful. Time to time if we catch them well before they hit the ground, they giggle and applause, and some time they threw more other items.

There was a US military base at the site of the Wonju Theater, and a field supply warehouse. There was a sewer underneath. After crawling from the entrance of the sewer for about 10 minutes, there is a manhole cover which opens to near the main warehouse. But only one person can crawl in or out. The village boys were in and out the sewer one by one at a time, and it was transported by relay. At the end, everyone shares evenly. The stealing was not right, we all knew. But there was not enough food, so the action was for the survival of the town folks.

War would bring great calamity.

A few days later, a friend of mine told me that all the refugees were going back home. I was happy to go back to my hometown too. On the river, the ice began to melt, and people were crossing the river in the boat. The next day, we packed everything we needed, went to the river, got on the boat, crossed the river safely, and returned to Wonju at last. But my house was gone, so I stayed with my older brother. When I got home, my brother, Do-shik, also returned home. When I went to the marketplace, all the stores and everything else were very badly damaged. The war brought such great calamity.

From then on, I had no choice but to go around looking for food. I began to wander near the US military base. When a friend of mine asked me if I would like to try to do the business of shoeshine, adding that it was pretty good job. I decided to get into that business. A naughty boy who had never polished his own shoes until then decided to work hard for the business for the American soldiers. However, my income was not so good, so I thought about robbing the US supply truck.

Before going through Hoeng-seong and Hong-cheon, there is Sammachi Pass and 99 S Type Pass, a very winding road. Trucks loaded with supplies had to slow down and crawl around the road. Hiding at the foot of the mountain, when a truck came, I jumped on it, picked up a supply box without the driver's notice, and threw it into the valley of the Sammachi Pass, Hong-cheon. Then, the people on the ground waiting would bring them to the village. There were all sorts of things in the supplies. One time, I noticed that a box was quite heavy, and I found out that it was frozen pork. The income for this stealing was much better than that of shoeshine business.

When I went to the Sammachi Pass again, but I couldn't do that any longer because the US military and Korean military police were escorting them. As this can no longer be done, after thinking about what to do, I thought that the liquor selling might be worthwhile. When I asked a boy who was in the liquor business already what kind of liquor was selling best. He told me to get the bellflower bland whiskey. That brand was sold three times the price he bought. I went to the market, bought 3 bottles of bellflower whiskey, went to the side of the barbed wire of the US military base and shouted "Hey, buy bellflower whiskey!" Some soldiers came without hesitation, and they gave me money and I gave them the whiskey through the wire fence. After selling 3 bottles in a few hours, I was blown away. I traded whiskey almost every day ever since, and the fun of making money was pretty good. I spent the money for my family, buying food for the family. In fact, it seems that I almost did the work of household pillar. One day I went near a barbed wire fence to sell whiskey. A black man came near and shot me with a slingshot (rubber gun). I was hit in the forehead and collapsed. I did not know how long the time passed, I woke up and saw that the whole place was white, and I was lying in bed. In the meantime, the Korean interpreter and the American soldier were chatting about what was going on, and he asked me if I was okay as I was awake. I didn't say anything. I thought about living for a while. The Americans looked quite tall that impressed me but nothing else.

A House boy

When I awoke from the injury from the sling shot a soldier said someone saw the scene where a sling shot hit me from a jeep moving toward the camp. The soldier picked me up and took me to the field hospital. He was the battalion commander, a lieutenant colonel, of the unit which was the soldier who shot me also belonged to. I told him I didn't have parents and I was just an orphan. The American soldier said that I could be his houseboy if I wanted. He was very kind to me. Thinking he was not only kind but also handsome. I nodded. After a couple of days rest for the recuperation, he told me to come back to the base. I nodded agreeing.

So, I became a US Army houseboy. He gave me a bed in the room next to the battalion commander to sleep in, so I slept there, and when it was time to eat, I ate at the officer's cafeteria, and there was so much to eat. If there was always a lot of food left. I asked if I could take the food in the can to my home, I was approved and I swept it into a bucket and brought it home in the battalion commander's car. My family ate well for a while. I was grateful for all this, so I bought a large bottle of makgeolli, Korean wine and gave it to the battalion commander, John, and he drank a cup of makgeolli and said, "very good". After that, I brought a bottle of makgeolli from time to time for him.

In return, he gave me a lot of chocolate, ration boxes, cigarettes, etc. One day, an old friend of mine came over to the barbed wire fence. I was glad to see him. But I realized that I was already in 6th grade, and I should return to the school. So, I got a headache and asked what to do. I got an application for returning to the school. I went to the school and talked to the teacher, and he made a document for me, so I went to middle school with it and told me to come by a few days. It was done. I paid the tuition and for books,

I wanted to go to the US with the US military

After thinking about it, I went to the market to tell my father. My father said that I need money to go to middle school, so he said, 'you can't.' I'm learning business here, and while I was struggling with the new job, a pretty lady came up to me one day and asked what my name was. She said her name was Kim Chae-bong and she was my stepmother. Hearing that, I laughed out loud. My father's wife was here again. So, the woman asked where my other stepmother was. I said there were two more, and her face turned blue. After that, I thought it must have been quite difficult for my father.

There were two mothers, Daebongi, the eldest mother, and the mother of Geumsik other than my real mother, as there were three wives of my father. With the help of Mrs. Kim Chae-bong, I paid the tuition of the middle school. This stepmother was very smart and excellent in management of disasters, and she was the one who raised our fortune. It was like finding a useful wife for my father. Until the second year of middle school, I got along well without any trouble, but the US military said that they were going to their home country. I was also asked to go with them, so I said yes. I went home and told my aunt about it, but the first word was 'No!' So, I asked why. She said that American soldiers take Korean children and throw them into the Pacific Ocean for ancestral rites. She emphasized again 'absolutely no', so I had many nights of drowning in the Pacific Ocean in my dreams. I eventually gave up the idea of going to America. The unit of the American soldier I became befriended with went back home at last. I felt so sad that I cried so sadly for the first time.

Brother Yoon-sik Came back home

One day, Yoon-sik, one of my brothers came back home. He said that he was caught with the national army. He emphasized the experience of starving for several days. Then, he said they sent him home. I think he would have lived if he had eaten properly, but my family kept giving him unconditionally to eat a lot. None the less, he died. I thought he died because he ate too much in short time. I knew that if a starving person suddenly overeats, he will die. He and I have been close since we started playing together, and it was very sad. He left the big house in the second year of middle school and moved to the house in Pyeongwon-dong. A new house was built in Pyeongwon-dong. It became a new home full of love. My stepmother also lived in the market area and my father moved in with her. My stepmother ran the store with my father for several years and ran a good business.

This store became the largest in the market. It was a large building with 25 doors. When the store was closing in the evening, I went to the store and helped closing for the night. Mainly, the second older brother, Bong-sik, did heavy staff, Bong-sik brother was paid for the work, I don't know why Bong-sik brother received money by what authority, but it was interesting to me then. But he also gave me though small portion of the money. The items mostly handled in the store were cauldrons for rice cooking. Many houses had no cauldrons because they were often destroyed by bombing. My father's tactics were excellent, I thought. He bought a lot of items such as pots in Seoul and transported them to Wonju Station by train.

After the war, I returned to my usual life as an early teen and went through a hardship as I passed through a period which was quite chaotic in my life. However, looking back 70 years later, I thought that I was fortunate enough to have survived such difficult periods relatively well. Going to school was a very different story though. I didn't have money to buy books, notebooks, or pencils, so it was difficult for me to study. It seemed like I was just playing with my friends rather than studying in school. I want to tell the story of that period of my life as a child in the period when everything was lacking.

I was earnestly wishing to grow into a person who loved the neighbors and helps the society by conserving supplies and working hard while thinking of difficult times. No matter how difficult the environment is, if I work hard every day with hope, eventually good days will come, that I believed firmly. I felt like I was living in a dark period then where I couldn't know the next day. But now that I think about it, I want to thank God for living as happily as I do today after doing my best every day throughout my life. I think everything is by God's grace.

A gangster became an agricultural doctor.

Currently, I live in the suburbs of Washington D.C and run a 50-acre farm that grows mushrooms and other crops. Also, 20 years ago, I received my PhD in Agriculture from the Pacific Western university, USA. I was acting like a gangster once when I was very young and a bad student in a small town. I was a human being who would have lived an unhappy life if I continued like the life of a gangster, but I returned to Catholicism by the grace of God, doing volunteer work as much as possible and helping neighbors. As a person who was once starving due to the 6.25 Korean War and was not able to pay even meager tuition on time, now I am satisfied with my current life and am happy. I am living well, thanks to God.

625, the Korean War

Chang-Wuk Kang, M.D.

On Sunday morning, June 25, 1950

I made a promise with kids in my neighborhood to go fishing on Sunday morning of June 25, 1950. It was a bright early summer day. I was 12-year-old and was in the second grade in middle school. The fish in the steam were abundant though they were small, and we were able to catch them easily and have fun. While we were picking up those fishes from the stream which ran under the main boulevard near my home, something struck our attention. We noticed several truckloads of soldiers were carried somewhere. It was unusual scene and draw our attention certainly. I have never seen so many trucks carrying so many soldiers, particularly the Korean Army. The soldiers were all armed and were in combat fatigue. It was unusual because I had never known that there were so many Korean soldiers at one time, and I never heard any of Korean Army was in fight with anyone. I was also very curious why all of them in several truck loads were moving on the Sunday morning. When I returned home for lunch, I mentioned what I saw. My father looked very serious but would not say a word in response to what I said about the truck load of the soldiers.

I then forgot the whole thing until a few days later when my eldest brother was trudging in through the front door of the house, a travel bag in one hand and holding one of my nephews by the other hand. All his family followed, my sister-in-law, two nieces and two nephews. They all looked blank in their expression and haggard. My mother could not hold her tears and went down in bare foot to the door and held her little grand kinds one by one. Then, she ran into the kitchen obviously to prepare the meals for them. That meal could have been neither breakfast nor lunch. My mother as usual must have thought about feeding kids like feasts. When the table was set, and meals were put on the table, the cranking of the utensils with vessels was quite noisy. No one was speaking. My mother's tears did not stop while the whole family were busily moving their utensils between the dishes and their mouths. I just watched, only thinking that I will have a wonderful time with my nephews and nieces. I did not think how starved they were. I always thought that they were my best playmates. That was all very important to me.

They had wonderful life in Seoul before the event. My oldest brother was the head of the largest textile factory in Korea, in Seoul. As the war started, he left everything with the plant, the largest textile factory in Korea and his beautiful home. In one small room of my home, the whole family of my brother's slept, two adults and four children. I still cannot figure out how they managed. One of the most painful things I discovered was that the executive of one of the largest textile factories in Korea suddenly has nothing to do but read the newspapers and listen to the radio news, and then facing the meal tables three times a day.

I loved my oldest brother. He was twenty years older than I was. I was like his child rather than his youngest brother, and he treated me like that also. Every time he visited us, he had never forgotten to bring a nice gift for me before the war. Though I was young to appreciate what was taking place he looked sad even to my eyes. I was mumbling in my head 'dear brother, don't worry! You do not have to worry about my gift this time!' It was very hard to imagine that I had to do something for my big brother, but I do not know what it should be.

One day I thought I did not see my second oldest brother for a few days or few weeks. It was not unusual as he time to time took night duties. He was a local police officer, but he was moved to what they called a 'combat police'. When I think about it, it was quite a funny name. He had a separate home since he got married. I saw him several weeks later when he knocked on my door early in the morning, about 4:00 AM. I was awakened but my mother opened the door. There, this brother of mine stood at the door in full battle fatigue, the helmet on his head, a rifle still hanging on his shoulder, but I could not recognize him by his face. I realized his face was covered with blood clots. In fact, I was frightened by the look of his face as his face was thickly covered with blood clots, and I could barely see his eyes. It appeared that he just returned home directly from the battle front of the Nackdong River, where one of the fiercest fights, the last bastion of South Korean military, took place. Enormous losses of life were taking place there in the early phase of the war. In fact, that defense line secured the small bastion of the Korean peninsula for the North Korean invasion. This front with prolonged stalemate was considered fiercest during the Korean war and loss of lives of both sides were enormous. But this protected the small area of the bastion in the southeast corner of the country. Well, I would like to say it saved the country. If the allied forces had even small setback at this front the Korean peninsula should have been overtaken by the North Korean forces, meaning there would have been no South Korea. This front saved enough time for the famous operation by the landing of Inchon under the command of General MacArthur. The communist rival was pushed back to the north quickly. No sooner the allied forces reached Yalu River, the Chinese army entered the war, and they quickly crossed the Yalu River. The massive human wave, literally, could not be resisted, and thus the allied forces were once again pushed back to below the original 38th parallel. The situation caused a much larger population of refugees in the south by this time. All over sudden, my hometown, Busan, became a melting pot of not only Korean from the whole areas of the north and the many foreigners as the allied forces joined the war. Again, I was too young to recognize this huge and complex situation of my hometown, Busan. I was fascinated by so many dialects by the those from many provinces and so many languages of so many countries that I have never seen or heard before. My hometown became one of the most bustling towns and instantaneously became an international city. I wonder if any city of the world was made up of so many people from so many different countries in such a short time. If America was called a melting pot, the Busan was a transient melting pot in 1950. As curious youth as I was, it stimulated my curiosity more.

I was in the second grade of Busan Middle School, in Choryang, Busan, Korea. In September 1950, about three months after the start of the hostility in the Korean Peninsula, I had a message from my school from a boy I have never met. He said the school principal asked us, the students at the school, to come to his home, not the school. We knew that the school campus was occupied by the soldiers of allied forces. Well, the school principal, Mr. Haduck Kim, announced the gathering of about two dozen students that he was going to open school classes in his backyard. I don't remember how I felt about the idea. But I was simply obedient to the teachers, any teacher. It was the first teaching and rule of my conduct from my father. Mr. Kim, the principal of Busan Middle School was able to bring in teachers in English, Korean languages, science, and mathematics. In fact, there were plenty of good candidates as teachers among those refugees who freed from Seoul, the capital where most of good colleges were located and many good scholars from the north. So many qualified teachers could be chosen from the streets of the city of Busan as they had no place to go or work. We started class in the middle of September 1950. The school eventually was able to obtain small land on the hill of the Busan reservoir and several U.S. Army tents. We then had full school, and we had many overqualified teachers. We had a very good education. Some of the classes were as good and qualified as those of good colleges. It was truly 'luck in misfortune.' My class were able to enter the best university, as many as any famous high school, years later. Among the classmates there were some from Seoul and North, meaning there also were many good classmates among us. Well, this opportunity opened my eyes too. It was indeed 'a blessing in disguise.' I had a very good education and was able to enter a top-notch University. When the war stopped by cease fire in 1953, the education came on the normal tract and the education was good enough that I was able to come to the United State for furthering my training in medicine. United Sates provided massive and detailed assistance for the educations in addition to many material and social assistance. We also had many western Christian missionaries who engaged us and taught good native English. The help from United States and countries supported the allied forces were incalculable.

My oldest brother and his family eventually returned to Seoul; he rebuilt the factory in no time with better machines and rebuilt another factory in another town. Textile production became vibrant. Meanwhile my father passed away at the age of 61. With the help of one of my sister-in-low, the youngest, my mother was able to manage her life and health. I owe a lot to this youngest sister-in-law who stayed with my mother building her family with my brother and four nieces. I came to America and married my wife in New York in the historical church in uptown New York.

Many of Korean in my age remember the hardship by the Korean War. But I found the hardship opened many opportunities to rebuild the country with new shape and dug out many potentials and accepted opportunities. When the country started a new direction after the military coup in 1961, somehow the country became more organized. The government encouraged young people to get educations from overseas, particularly United States. One thing for sure; by the military coup the country was run by the military officers who were all graduates from military academy and their education and training systems were all from American systems. Many officers had training in United States. When I resumed my medical educations in United Sates, it was not that difficult except the conversational language. Without good facility we must have had very good education and we had minimal hardship in engaging in American medical system.

Yes, I might have had some difficulty and had my share of hardship through my three brothers suffering due to the combat, one emotionally and the other physically, and abandoning his huge factory and home but I would not say I had severe hardship by the Korean War personally. In fact, I have more enjoyable memories. We still call it '625.' In fact, I still think the war was a war that certainly caused severe hardship, trauma, and sad memory for many, but I would say it also altered the direction of Korea for the better although the fruit came later. The international Olympic was held very first time in Korea in 1988. The potential of the Koreans was widely cultivated to the extent that we now see the Korea in the economical rank of 12th in the world, preparing to send the rocket to the moon, building major structures in all over the world, became a major exporter of automobiles and shipbuilding as building the largest tanker. It was ranking 125 at the end of the 625 in terms of the economic strength. While many of my friends and acquaintances might have different memories than mine, I do not believe it came from my naive optimism or ignorance. My optimism came from the budding new country after the unbearable hardship by the Korean War. When we gained the freedom from the Japanese occupation, the colonialism, we could not do much to rebuild the country for fifteen years but there was dramatic change after the military coup in 1961. In 1988, the Republic of Korea opened the International Olympic Game in Korea which was enormous opportunity for the Korea to be known all over the world, better than what Korean war did. In 2020 the Republic of Korea gained the ranking of 12 in economy in the world. When I toured in Europe about ten years ago, I was shocked by the ubiquitous signboards of Korean products in many European cities. Oh! I was enslaved by my love of 'Made in U S A' in my childhood. The tragic Korean War that we call '625' certainly was a turning point for the Korean future which they are enjoying. What surprise me is that the Korean became more optimistic. I grew up in ever pessimistic society. I can see that well because I was away from Korea during the transition while those who witnessed the transition were in Korea enjoying the blossom and now, they are taking this huge gain and growth for granted.

Epilogue

Se-Woong Ro/ Poet

Every year on June 25th, I am reminded of how North Korean leader Kim Il-sung pushed down South Korea and occupied Seoul in 3 days 72 years ago. Students in Korea now say that they do not know who started the Korean War.

The generation that experienced the 6.25 war is leaving this world and going to heaven one by one. The number of people who remember the war is leaving us every year. Poet/Professor Choi Yeon-Hong, who edited and published the first two books entitled 'the forgotten war 6.25, 1950' The book was created by him with me. He passed away two years ago. Now all that's left is the book publication, which needed to be finalized. But there was still work to be done. I wish to preserve the history and the story of the experiences of those who were in the war or affected by the war, remember the story, so that all the generations should know the history. This third publication with same title, Volume 3, is being prepared as I wished to complete before June 25th of 2023. I want to weave the experiences of various people and leave them in this world. So that history will never be forgotten.

There are many people who go to heaven after the age of 80. 625 Experience Generations are now over 90 years old. Only long-lived people remain. Kyung-Ju Lee, president of the Korean War Veterans Association, also passed away from laryngeal cancer while writing the manuscript for the third volume. Former chairman of Korean War Veterans Association Lee Byung-Hee, the retired army lieutenant colonel, also said that he would write a manuscript, but he passed away much sooner. I planned to collect 6.25 experiences from as many as I could, but I included those as best I could collect in Volume 3.

I would like to continue collecting manuscripts and publish one book every year if possible and to continue as long as my health permits. It is said that when the experiences of many people come together, it becomes preservable history. Everyone will have to work together to make history.

On the other hand, there are still a lot of people who went through the pain of that time together during the uprising, so I am very careful and worried that there may be something that will put a burden on me. But I think these records are a matter beyond the personal level. The 6.25 uprising is a historical fact at the level of the nation that goes beyond the realm of mere personal experience. Furthermore, it is a problem of high-level that requires deep and fundamental reflection on human behavior such as war.

I believe that suffering must be thoroughly overcome to achieve the maturity of a nation or individual or consciousness. Thorough overcoming suffering does not mean concealing or avoiding suffering. The question of who first committed the 6.25 uprising was also announced in the newspapers at this time, but just because it is revealed does not mean that our suffering will be overcome. To what extent would you have been a slave to a collective ideology and aimed your gun at your own people? Why do humans have to go to war? I think the answer should be obtained from the fundamental question. What can compensate for the suffering of the 6.25 uprising, when the entire nation was bleeding and suffocating? There will be no reward except for the whole nation to be reborn into spiritual maturity.

War is man's madness and disease. As time passes, it appears to have healed on the surface, but if there is no fundamental healing, it may burst when and where. Humans are always forced to choose between peace and war. Through this book, I think it is necessary to give the younger generation who have not experienced turmoil an indirect experience.

Forgotten War 1950

In Their Adolescence

Remembered by 8 Octogenarians

Third Edition June 6, 2023

Editors: Dr. Chang-Wuk Kang / Se-Woong Ro

Published by KDP.Amazon

Design & Publishing: Song Yoon/Sam Ro

Email: cwkang@comcast.net or swro0403@gmail.com

Printed in the U.S.A.